# GOD'S
# ROMANTIC
# GETAWAY

*Be encouraged
as you need
Love Jemma
God Bless*

by
Jemma Regis

Christian Fiction

Published by Conscious Dreams Publishing

ISBN: 978-1-907402-58-6

Cover Design: Jemma Regis and Martin Finnegan
www.definedimagery.com

# Contents

# Acknowledgements

I cannot begin this without acknowledging my Father in Heaven. He took my brokenness and made me whole. I now know what it means to be truly saved, for He has transformed my life in such a way, it leaves me confident of His love for me. His faithfulness, patience and love take my breath away.

Along this journey, He has sent others to help and guide me and I would like to thank them for assisting Him in getting me to this point.

Derrick Brown — your help in the writing of this book was inspirational and challenging. Thank you for bringing out the writer in me.

Dee Anderson — your encouragement and support has covered me and pushed me when I needed to be. Your help was definitely Spirit led.

Joanne Oliver — Your input in the editing was beyond a blessing.

Marcus Johnson — for your help with copyright. Having the lyrics to the songs incorporated into the book was very important to me and you helped make it possible. God, bless you.

Martin Finnegan — your gift of shooting the front cover may well have saved me hundreds of pounds, but what I am most thankful for is your willingness and selflessness to help. I am no supermodel but you sure made me look good!

Pastor David Daniel and Pastor Joseph Daniel when God led me to your fellowship I had no idea I would be under the guidance of such humble leaders. Thank you for leading me, covering me and trusting in me. Pastor David, we have had many, many debates but you have always believed in me and never doubted God's call on my life. Thank you for never giving up on me.

Pastor Freddie Brown — Thank you for being there in those midnight hours, when I had more questions than answers. I could never repay you for the hours you spent counselling me.

Pastor Sheila Belgarve — From the day you read the first draft you have stood my me and supported me, working away to get this story out to as many as would hear it. I am so grateful for your support.

Minister Verna Walsh — Your, support, prayers and love from across the seas have been such a blessing. Thank you!

To my PCF (People's Christian fellowship) family, you have shown your love in so many ways. To those who have encouraged and expressed their excitement for the release of this book, thank you so much, it means a lot to me.

Joan Williams — for the hours you spent listening and counselling, thank you!

Bev and Garfield Bowen, Keisha Jackson, Cookie Goodrich, Thelma Brown, Deborah Grey, Recci Gibbs, Carol Valentine, Jason & Samantha Boothe, Carl Regis, Karen Nell, thank you for welcoming me into your homes during my sabbaticals.

Tony & Joan de- Pass, forever faithful, dear friends.

Gail Peters, there are no words; you have seen the good, the bad and the ugly. I thank God for you, without your kindness and love, I do not know how I would have come through. God truly has blessed you with a generous heart of love.

To my siblings, Judie, Josephine, Jael & John, your patience and support over the years has been priceless. Josephine, thank you for your help with the cover design.

To my father, John Regis, I thank God for you and for and all you have taught me.

Lastly but by no means least to my mother, you will forever be in my heart. I am more like you than I had realised, which means you taught me well. I just wish you were here to see this and hold a copy in your hand.

*Love Jemz, x*

# Foreword

I pastor a church in Tottenham, North London, England. It is a vibrant, family oriented church, situated in the heart of one of London's most popular boroughs. Our church relies heavily on the gifting and service of its members and I am so encouraged because God has blessed us with extremely talented and willing people, who have served to elevate the profile of our fellowship and allowed us to impact people's lives all over the world, with the gospel of Jesus Christ.

Prior to Jemma taking up membership in our fellowship, I knew her as a believer through my association with the church she attended. However, I also recognised her as a successful businesswoman who ran a highly regarded catering business called 'Jems Caterers'. Whenever 'Jems caterers' were attending to the food at a wedding or special function, you knew the food would look and taste exquisite and you could be confident that the service would be professional and of the highest standard. However, at this point I need to be excused for just one moment. Her food tastes so good. Yes, I must admit, I am guilty on occasions of forgetting my etiquette and upbringing. On numerous occasions I have had to mentally restrain myself in public, from tearing into the food like I am at my mum's house on a Sunday afternoon. Jemma is, without doubt, an accomplished and gifted chef and I have been blessed. I really have been blessed.

Jemma seemed to be someone who had it all going for her — she had purchased her own home, had a nice car, always dressed well and so outwardly, she appeared to be confident and strong. She also has a kind heart and was someone others would turn to for advice. This was the side of Jemma that the world saw. When she started to attend our fellowship, she came to see me for pastoral care. I had several sessions with her and was allowed to see the real person hidden behind the mask. This young lady had numerous challenging issues which she struggled with and was in need of help. She was dealing with disappointment, depression, hopelessness and regret and I sensed that she was desperate for a breakthrough but she could not see how s he would achieve it.

Over the years and amidst her challenges, I saw growth but Jemma sometimes struggled to see it in herself. It was evident she loved the Lord but struggled to love herself. In my opinion, Jemma is a fighter and I watched her fight through her obstacles. She started setting her alarm clock to wake up early every morning because she had a most important meeting, a meeting with God. She became excited and enthusiastic about her times with the Lord, He was delivering her from the darkness of depression and she was experiencing His joyous victory on a daily basis.

I liked what I was seeing and because I knew her experience would be a great help to other believers, I gave her opportunities to share and inspire others to develop their relationship with Him also. What she was experiencing, I knew most Christians needed. For a while things were going well and then gradually I began to see another change. Jemma was at war within. She had set high standards for her walk with Christ and desired to live up to those standards but her failures left her devastated and with that devastation, came taunts from her past.

In 2011, she informed me that she was going away for two months. She was desperately seeking intimacy with God. Only this time she didn't want it to be a cycle like before, she wanted something permanent. A breakthrough from the chains bound around her feet, that every so often tripped her up. I have never seen her as broken, depressed and desperate as she was and you could tell that this was a woman on a mission. A woman after God's own heart.

Upon her return, she met with me and I saw a completely different person. Jemma had changed, she had a reason to live and there was a smile on her face. The dynamics of our meetings shifted and it was incredible. The transformation which took place in her was nothing short of a miracle. The Lord had expelled the darkness and this was a new day. What happened was more than the commencement of a new chapter; it was an entire new book.

The means for Jemma's change was quite simple and has always been accessible to every born again believer. Her perspective on life changed, she started listening out for and to the Lord intensively and through this is developing a very intimate relationship with Him and is captivated by His revelations. She also reads the bible in a new light and is developing a mature appreciation for its application and becoming passionate in her discovery.

Now she has come to the point where she has documented a more recent part of her story and she is calling it 'God's Romantic Getaway'. I would suggest that this part of her life, which you are about to read, is most beneficial to the body of Christ. It is an honest, inspirational testimony. She would admit — I know — to many challenges along the way, some ups and downs, some victories and some failures, but for Jemma, her walk with Christ has become real and meaningful because her priority is to please the Lord. Jemma is an ordinary believer who struggles with the same things most believers struggle with but she has found something that has given her faith super new meaning. This book will inspire you. I admit that it could leave you feeling that something is missing in your life but Jemma shows how obtainable this is.

I highly recommend this inspiring book. Still there are two areas that I would like to comment on. One challenge for me was the use of Jemma's language. It is no secret I like football, I like action movies, I like westerns and in my dreams, I am a Bear Grylls action man — hero type — survival bloke. My wife loves the romantic movies and I watch them with her because of my deep love for her. However, given the choice, I would find some pleasure running barefoot over a very large termite's mound, shouting at the top of my voice: "I love myself, I love myself, I love myself." So, in saying that, as I read this book there were sentences that Jemma used which made me shift in my chair a little. When I spoke to Jemma about this, it amused her. Still I guess it is not too dissimilar in language as that found in the bible in the 'Song of Solomon.' This is her personal, genuine account as to how her relationship with the Lord has developed and it is one to be desired.

One other thing to note is this — Jemma found her meeting place — a place of retreat which she was comfortable with. It doesn't mean that everyone has to leave the country to hear from the Lord; what is being promoted is the wonderful ideal of taking time out exclusively to be in the presence of the Lord and I hope that every reader senses the Lord's call to make this practice their habit.

My final two words are these: "inspirational" and "hopeful." This book will inspire you to pursue a closer and deeper personal relationship with Jesus. Jemma is an ordinary young woman who has and continues to, experience something most wonderful. She extends the hope that everyone can get there too. When you read this book, you should read it with this in mind. It is like Brother Lawrence's little book called "The practice of the presence of God" which leaves you feeling that the principles and practices presented, are accessible. It is so simple: just talk to the Lord and be sure of this, He is right there wanting to speak with you.

*Pastor David Daniel*

# Introduction

You are probably still uncertain as to why you have settled down to read this book. Perhaps you glimpsed its chapters, scanned the contents and thought, "this could be an easy read." Maybe it was the title that caught your attention, or was it a gift? Maybe it was recommended to you or you happened to stumble upon it. Whatever the reason, I expect you are wondering what you will gain from its contents.

Will it fulfil your desire for knowledge, help or support? Is it going to meet the needs you have and offer the answers you are in search of, or at least point you in the right direction?

Is it going to challenge you, educate or inspire you?

If any such thoughts are running through your mind, do not worry. I often feel the same way when I start reading a book and as bold as it may sound, I believe this book will do many of the above and possibly more.

The purpose for my writing began as inserts in my personal journal, until one day whilst making an entry,

God spoke to me and told me I needed to publish my writing. From that point on, my thoughts changed from me to us — we — and you.

Often people only get to know you personally through one on one encounters, as we share with those closest to us personal areas of our lives. Well, I had had many one to one encounters with my journal; it was the place I released my joys, fears and thoughts. It was the place I poured out my heart to God in praise, anger and even frustration.

Until now, it was my place. I have now opened it up by inviting you to join me on a very personal journey, so throughout various chapters you will find extracts from my journal, which means I will sometimes write in past tense, sometimes in present tense. You will invariably sometimes feel as though you are in 'the moment' with me and at others, as I reflect back, as though you are reading my account of past events.

Whatever your reasons are for reading this book, you are about to encounter 'my place.' I would like to take you on a journey, a real-life journey filled with everyday occurrences that affect the way we think, behave and interact with others. This is a journey that opened the eyes of my heart and altered the patterns of my life. Whether you realise it or not, you are already on a journey but I would like you to take some time out to accompany me on mine, in the hope that it will assist you on yours. As I share my reflections with you, I encourage you to take your own reflective pit-stops, at times guiding you to certain scripture, or certain activities. This guidance is not intended to be prescriptive but are to serve as encouragement, as you are exposed to the insights I have gained.

I was a young woman who loved God and more than anything I desired to please Him.

My relationship with Him was real and living and not built on a foundation of just attending church. I read my bible regularly and I believed I had had enough encounters with God to know that He was real. However, with all the best intentions and spiritual insight, my happiness in Him was always short lived. Having encountered Him in such powerful ways, I should have been up there walking strong like Paul but instead I was living more like Elijah, whilst he hid out in the cave (1 Kings 19).

I was a child of God who was desperate, depressed and weary. I often felt hopeless, emotionally drained, invisible and somewhat at a loss. I knew what I wanted but struggled to connect with it.

Maybe you have been there yourself at some point?

I grew up in church and was baptised at the age of thirteen. My friends and family would probably describe me as a committed Christian and though that all sounds rosy, being a Christian has had its struggles causing me at times to doubt God's very existence. This is probably because for a long while I didn't really know what being a Christian truly entailed.

I tried to live as the bible taught and was always helping others, so why was I still searching and why did I feel desperate, invisible, lost, depressed but most of all, a disappointment to God?

If, like me you are a Christian who has a heart for God and have or periodically experienced any one or more of set backs I have described, then I invite you to accompany me on this getaway. If you are desperate, hurting, exhausted and in need of help, with no idea where to turn or who to turn to, I urge you to join me. If on the other hand, you are at a point where you desire to take your relationship with God to another level and are not quite sure how to go about it, come join me and I will show you what I had to do to break through and soar.

Before we leave I must point out that I am the type of person who likes to keep things real and if I am going to read a book it has to be real and I have to able to identify with it. So just in case you are thinking this may not be the book for you, or you are tired of reading and want something tangible, I hear you and it does not get more tangible than this. I invite you to drop your load and join me and do not worry about bringing anything because where we are going everything you will need is already there and when it is time to leave, you may not even want to leave!

I am going to take you behind the scenes of my life, spanning a period of approximately twelve years, during which time I was privileged to embark on two spiritual sabbaticals that turned my life inside out. Though the trips had similarities, they were also incredibly different.

However, the outcome of both left me exposed to the person God had created me to be. The question was, was I ready to be that person?

The six years between the two trips were by far the loneliest years of my life, which is not surprising, given their nature. The bible is full of documented evidence of prophets being whisked away on visions and men being saved from a fiery furnace and the mouths of lions, seas parting and more. All through the Scriptures, God is interacting with His chosen vessels in real and practical ways and we wonder why we are not seeing or experiencing similar things today. After all, God has not changed.

Well believe it or not, on my trips, that is precisely how it was with me and God. God had called me away and was exposing Himself to me in ways that were very much on par with men and women in the bible and what child of God does not want to be in that position?

Although I was baptised at the age of thirteen, if I am honest, my real walk with God began when I was seventeen, following the death of my mother. Losing mummy left me at a crossroads, where my choices were either God...... or whatever else was out there. I chose God but with no real solid foundation, 'whatever else was out there' argued a strong case and thus my struggle as a young Christian began.

As a vulnerable young woman, "the world" as older Christians called it, offered me counterfeit comforts that I did not find in the Church and by counterfeit, I mean unsatisfactory contentment. Church on the other hand, captivated me, stirring up a desire to know God, want God and have Him close by but each service I attended left me thinking there had to be more to God than just church. The problem was, I had grown up thinking that being a Christian meant going to church and I was already doing that.

Over the years my search for more than just "church" left me saddened and hungry, as I constantly hit dead ends. I sang in the choir, taught Sunday school and offered my services where required but inside I was still yearning for more.

I made lots of mistakes, took many wrong turns, ignored signs, drove through red lights and halted at green ones before I realised being a Christian did not just mean going to church. Being a Christian was a lifestyle that involved having a relationship with God. God wanted to be part of my life, He wanted to have conversations with me, hang out with me, laugh and cry with me. He wanted to be my everything; He wanted to be my big brother, my father, friend, confidant, lover, helper, carer, provider and everything else a relationship brings. He did not just want to be a being that I worshipped with no intimacy. The older generation were always saying God had not changed; He is the same yesterday, today and forever. That being the case why wasn't His input in my life the same as those I read about in the bible. Well, it was my desire to know as much as was humanly possible about the God who had not changed. I too wanted to experience Him like the patriarchs, prophets, disciples and everyday people in the bible. I wanted to speak and have Him respond. I wanted to sense His presence and be stilled by it. I wanted to be hushed by Him and have Him change the format of my day just because He chose to. I wanted a relationship with God and not just to be acquainted with Him and the best part was He had placed those desires in my heart because He wanted the same for me.

Up until this point my life had been filled with so many emotional ups and downs that stemmed from an unstable childhood, damaged emotions and a distorted mindset. All of which I carried around without realising. The highs were governed by my times with God and short lived moments of joy, whilst the lows were bombarded with taunting thoughts of past hurts and acts of abuse from my early childhood, that I struggled to let go of and which you can read more about in my next book, 'A Precious Stone'.

Just for the record, there is nothing significantly special about me; I am an ordinary person with a desire for intimacy with God. So now you know a little about me, I think it is time we got going.

We begin our journey in 2004, ten months prior to my first sabbatical and two years after my return from Orlando, Florida where I had worked for eighteen months. This was a time in my life when all was well and I thought all my prayers had been answered.

So often we think we have control over our lives but in reality, our lives are in God's hands. It is His purpose and not our plans, that will be accomplished in our lives.

*"Many are the plans in a person's heart, but it is the Lord's purpose that prevails."* (Pro 19:21 NIV)

*Why am I discouraged?*
*Why is my heart sad?*
*I will put my hope in God!*
*I will praise Him again – My Saviour and my God!*

PSALM 42:5 NLT

# 1

# The Beginning

My 5am prayer time was a strict regime I had set myself that instilled discipline. "Just five more minutes... No NOW!" was the daily pep talk I gave myself as the alarm went off.

In the quiet stillness of the morning before the hustle of the day began, I had an appointment with God and He was going to show up even if I did not. Of course, I was tempted to hit the snooze button and sometimes I did but the thought of God anticipating my arrival or feeling disappointed that I had not shown up, was enough to get me out of bed. It was nothing complicated, just a simple time of prayer and bible reading with no distractions, before I set off for work. During that time, I was learning how to communicate with God, to recognise His voice and the importance of obedience. Life was not perfect but my Christian walk was progressing and I was growing stronger in my faith and it was my faith that held me secure.

My confidence in God had excelled, given the fact that He had granted one of my long-time desires — marriage. Marriage was never my number one priority but it was something I desired and dreamt of and I was weeks away from becoming engaged to be married. It was a surreal time and I recall frequently pinching myself to make sure it was real.

I was getting married.

A dream that seemed so distant was coming to pass and I owed it all to God. Not only was I getting married, I was also moving to America. God had granted me two desires in one and I was humbly in awe of Him. Plans were in motion and I was excited. Sometimes, as I walked along the street, I often looked up to the sky and smiled, and my smile uttered a million "thank yous" that only God and I understood.

I awoke one Sunday morning in April 2004 to the most beautiful day — a cloudless blue sky and radiant sunshine. Whilst getting ready for church I reminisced on God's goodness to me as I anticipated the arrival of my fiancé-to-be the following month, for our planned engagement. The sun was shining so bright that it appeared to be smiling and I loved days like these because they reminded me of my time in Orlando.

I checked my watch, great, I had time for a quick call to the States before I left for church. It was the perfect time for a good morning call to the man I loved.

The phone rang for a short while and as always when he answered my heart skipped a beat. His voice sounded hollow, distant and shaky. Something was wrong. I no longer noticed the cloudless sky and the radiant sunlight that shone into my room; suddenly everything became overcast. And then it came the thing you think will never happen to you, if for no other reason than the expectation of God's protection. In one sentence, the engagement, plans for marriage, relationship and conversation was over!

First the shock, then the questions, followed by more shock and finally, pain.

It was a cruel joke, 'let's give her what she wants then just before she has a chance to hold it, whisk it away so quickly she scarcely has time to catch her breath'.

That is precisely how it felt.

I was in a daze but surprisingly still made it to church. I have no idea how I got there but told myself I would find peace in God's house. I do not recall what the message was about but I know it brought no peace or healing.

Now what? I felt lost and numb. I was living in a balloon of disbelief and when I climbed into bed later that afternoon, I stayed there for three days with no food or drink, just an endless flow of tears. My stomach was in knots, I had lost my appetite and I could not stop the pain.

After hitting a dead end at church, I was surprised to find that my only source of comfort came from God. I use the word 'surprise' because I never thought God could heal a heart that was as broken as mine. He was supposed to grant and protect my desires from being smashed to smithereens. He was supposed to protect me. I did not get answers to the million and one questions because I did not have a million and one questions, I only had one: "where did I go wrong?" I wanted to ask God to fix my situation. I wanted to beg Him to turn things around and allow my heart the privilege of embracing the joy it had once experienced. I wanted to get angry and ask God why but I could not find the words. I wanted it to be a dream but it was real.

My days were painful and my sleep too short. And when I awoke in the mornings, for the first few seconds I was free but then came the whirlwind of emotions, pain and accusations, bowling me over before I could even open my eyes wide enough to see the new day.

They say what does not kill you will make you stronger and I wasn't dead, so I had to find a way to live, breath and smile through my brokenness. The last time I had hurt this much was when my mum died. I had prayed for this, desired this, spent so many years alone and finally my prayer had been answered. I was happy — no — I was beyond happy, until it was all snatched away. My inside hurt and my heart felt like it had been ripped out, trampled upon and shattered into millions of pieces. All communication with the man I loved, the man I had planned to spend the rest of my life with, had been cut off. I tried to hold back from calling but maybe, just maybe, he would answer the phone. An explanation, an argument! I needed anything but the deafening silence.

"Hi, this is Mark. Please leave a message after the tone and I will get back to you."

It was his voice but not the response I was looking for.

Sleep became my place of escape because when I was sleeping I wasn't thinking, so I drank alcohol to help me sleep but that left me feeling guilty, raising questions of my faith in God. I was hurting but what I wanted God to do and what I asked Him to do, were two different things. I wanted Him to make it all better so Mark and I could live happily ever after. Instead I pleaded with Him to rescue me from the negative thoughts that ran through my mind and shelter me from the pain that was too much for my body to contain.

The course He took was one I will never forget and I learned a very important lesson. I had to forgive! I had to forgive someone who broke my heart and refused to speak to me. I had to forgive when all I wanted to do was lash out and let Mark know how much he had hurt me. I had to forgive but I wanted him to feel as much pain as I was feeling. I had to forgive but I was the wronged party! Deep down I knew Mark was not a bad person; that it was not through lack of care that he did not contact me. I knew he had stuff he was dealing with but that did not make it any easier for me to bear.

My 5am prayer time turned into 24-hour prayer. I wanted to be whole again. My mind, body and spirit needed healing and nothing anyone said or did brought me solace. Like a victim running for their life from their predator, I ran into the arms of God for comfort and in His arms, is where I found the true meaning of Phil 4:7 NIV *And the peace of God, which surpass all understanding, shall keep your hearts and minds through Christ Jesus.*

Not only did God's peace surpass my understanding, it kept my mind free from the bombardment of emotional attacks, by channelling all my thoughts and energy through His peace.

The first thing I had to do was forgive. It was hard but forgiving meant letting go of my hurt and I began to understand the negative attachments behind not letting go. It didn't matter what Mark did or did not do, if I did not forgive him, I would remain bound and I needed to be free. All my life I had made forgiving harder than it needed to be, after all, why should anyone hurt me and get away with it? Forgiving them would mean it was ok and it was not ok. Using my present situation, God taught me that forgiving released me from the attachments that sought to corrode my inner peace, so I could live and release the other person to Him.

If I did not forgive, the only person I would be hurting was myself.

A good friend told me to take one minute at a time, and that is what I did. Thinking five minutes ahead was too painful and when the waves of emotions came knocking, I ran for my life to God and His word. God became my rock. His word became my foundation and I refused to let either of them out of my grip. The minutes turned to hours, the hours to days, the days to weeks and the weeks to months. I had never encountered the depth of security I felt during those painful months and I was not about to let it slip from my hands. God became my friend and in time I felt no anger or revenge towards Mark. Some would say I chose to blot out my pain but I know different. Blotting out could not produce the degree of love, joy and peace that I found during my dark hour.

In the midst of my pain, I became a rock and source of comfort to others but no one, other than my oldest sister and a very small circle of friends, knew of my situation.

Part of me was ashamed. I had nothing to be ashamed of but I could not bring myself to share my news until now. As time went on, I became stronger in the Lord and refused to entertain the devil's chatter, like his taunts that Mark did not care and had moved on. The situation placed a longing in my heart when I saw couples holding hands and the many weddings I attended. This included a friend who walked down the aisle to the same music I had chosen for my special day. When I heard the music my inside erupted but every time I felt challenged, I ran to God pleading His word over my mind. Repeating scriptures like "You will keep in perfect peace, whose mind is stayed on You because he trusts in You" (Isa 26:3 NKJV) I would squint my eyes and repeat it a million times if needed, until the tormenting thoughts in my mind were gone and God's peace resided in my heart.

To this day, I am amazed as to how I came through one of the most painful times of my life, but it propelled me to draw closer to God. I endured eight months of character building as God repositioned me. Eight months of growing, stretching and developing. Eight months of peace and joy in the midst of sadness.

## 2

# War Zones

That year I was due to spend Christmas in America. This was a trip that had been arranged and paid for before the break up. My flight was booked for Friday 17th December and about two months prior, I felt God speaking to me, urging me to leave my job. If I am honest, His announcement was no surprise.

My commitment to my morning devotions had caused me to draw closer to Him and with that closeness came a hunger for things I had not considered before and a drifting from things I was previously attached to. Then one morning in prayer, as I pondered over the changes that were happening, trying not to allow my mind to run wild, God informed me that when I left to go to America I was not to return to my job. Thursday 16th was to be my last day.

Some of you may be asking how did I know it was God speaking to me and how I recognised His voice? Well, I used to ask that same question when I heard people say God spoke to them. It's a question that is both complex and simple to explain.

When God speaks, it can be through a scripture that to an extent literally speaks directly to you, you read it and you just know deep within that it is for you. You recognise it in the same way you recognise someone is talking about you without actually saying your name. God can also speak to you from within. You can be going about your business and sense you need to change direction or you need to say or do whatever He is telling you. It is kind of like a feeling but with words; a still small voice. Another way God can speak to you is simply just to speak to you audibly, clear and precise. When God told me I was not to return to work, that is precisely what I heard as I was praying. It was not out loud so the person next to me could hear but it was loud enough for me to hear it and it definitely was not something I imagined.

There are many ways God can speak to you but unless you spend time getting to know Him, you will struggle to recognise His voice. Whatever way He chooses to communicate with you, He always sends His divine peace, which for me acts as His signature.

If you choose to obey, His peace is your sign you are on the right road. If you choose to do it your way, generally that peace is disturbed. When God spoke to me I knew I was hearing right and I knew I had to obey. At the time I had no concerns as to how I would manage financially but I did have concerns as to what God was asking me to do. He didn't just want me to leave my job, He wanted me to leave my job to prepare for ministry and I did not feel I was ministry material.

My obedience was anything but swift. On the one hand, I knew I had heard right but on the other I couldn't see myself in a ministerial role. Despite my delay, God had a plan and He was not playing! In an effort to help me on my way, things at work got so bad that if I did not leave of my own free will, they would have sacked me anyway. Overnight, management and staff turned against me and anyone who supported me was reprimanded for their stance. Work became a miserable place and one Friday afternoon when I could take it no more, I broke down and cried out to God for help. But God was silent. He was not ignoring me but I had been ignoring Him. I knew I had to hand in my notice but I had been procrastinating.

That weekend I made up my mind to leave my job but by Monday morning, I had come up with a plan that meant I would have to return to work in the New Year for two months, ensuring I had enough funds behind me. However, during the week, things at work escalated and by Thursday my resignation was on my Manager's desk.

My deliberation and delay meant that after my vacation, I would have had to return to work for one week, when God had been adamant that I was not to return at all. However even in my disobedience, He granted me favour and I was told there was no point in returning for that one week and as an act of goodwill, I would be paid for it.

That meant that when I left on Thursday December 16th, I never went back.

I would love to say it was a wonderful time in my life, where having witnessed how God had worked things in my favour, I was ready and raring to go! But it was not wonderful and I was not raring to go anywhere. I had just walked away from my full-time career as a chef, with no plans for my future and whilst my entire being was submerged in God's peace and I knew I was on the right road, I had no confidence in the vocation He was asking me to undertake.

My vacation was painful, as memories of my past relationship flooded my heart and mind. I thought of Mark and how he always met me at the airport, then drove me to my hotel. I remembered my anticipated excitement of spending time with him over the Christmas period; the thought of resting in his arms or holding hands as we walked and talked. Seeing his smile and embracing the love we shared. Often, as I dwelled on these thoughts, a momentary smile would appear on my face, only to be cut short.

That was then and this was now!

Upon my arrival, no one came to meet me at the airport and even though I knew Mark would not be there, part of me dreamt and longed that God would work a miracle and he would be waiting for me, smiling with open arms. I even found myself looking for him as I came through arrivals but he was not there. After a long wait, I collected my hired car and made my own way to the hotel. At home in London, I had adjusted and accepted the break-up but being back in Orlando, I was not doing so well. My mind was full of so many thoughts. My life had changed but for better or worse? I was on my own but should I have been on my own? I had left my job and I had no plans! One of the world's most organised women had no plans!

I called myself stupid, amongst other things I dare not repeat for leaving my job, to prepare for ministry of all things and spent most of my time in bed, feeling frightened and alone. My emotions were all over the place. Throughout all of this, God never moved His stance and deep down I knew I had not misunderstood His request — quite the opposite, it was what He had said that scared me. Other than His command, He had not given me one reason why I was ministry material but I had given Him a million as to why I was not.

My mind became a war zone; who would believe me? Why me? Did God really know me? What had I done to qualify for the role? What did I know about ministry? I was most definitely the wrong person for the job. Whilst my mind filled with reasons against, my heart ordered my steps. My steps were leading me to obedience and my obedience kept me in right standing with God but at the same time went against all human instinct and knowledge.

Christmas day came and I spent my time alone in a hotel room, crying and sleeping the hours away and eating cold leftovers from the night before. The Christmas before had been so different, as Mark and I made plans for our future; now all I had were memories and my memories were killing me. Being back in America was not helping.

After two weeks of misery, I returned home and made out like I had the time of my life. I tried to focus on what God had said but no matter how much I tried, I could not see myself through His eyes and felt by giving up my job, I had made the biggest mistake of my life. I have never been so certain, so scared and so uncertain about anything as I was back then. Memories mixed with pain, pain mixed with uncertainty, uncertainty mixed fear, fear mixed with hope and hope centred on God. I had His peace but I was not at peace. Upon my return, I spent a further two weeks in bed unable to motivate myself to do anything. Who was I kidding? God could not use me; I was tainted and biblically uneducated. I was nobody. Laying in bed, my days were spent thinking about what I had given up and once again, I was delaying God's instruction to go back to America for a further three months. Where would I stay? How would I manage financially? And what would happen in America that could not happen in London? So many questions, no answers but I still had His peace. What should have been a joyous time was a lonely and scary time and although I knew I had heard from God and had to get my act together, I was totally out of my comfort zone. I still prayed and I still had faith in God but I lacked confidence in myself.

The night I told my pastor what God had told me and His instructions for me, it took me an entire hour just to say the word 'ministry' and when I finally said it I then proceeded to tell him why I must have got it wrong, even though I knew I had not. My pastor believed God's word for me and that made things worse. "How can you be sure? Shouldn't you be telling me I need to go back and pray, or something along those lines? I am not biblically educated. I cannot go into ministry, I just can't!" My pastor listened and smiled as I reeled off all the reasons my flesh gave and then pointed out that despite my fears, I was still being obedient and he was confident God had not made a mistake.

Deep down I knew my pastor was right but I was too scared to accept and admit it and I did not think my family and friends would accept it either. My past did not qualify me to minister to others; I had far too many issues. I could not speak in public, neither had I studied theology or been to bible school. I was tainted by the many sinful mistakes I had made and I was insignificant. No one knew me and those who did know me, would laugh me to scorn.

Despite my turmoil, I did not have the heart to disobey God, His peace ordered my steps and I eventually booked my flight to America. Friends and family thought I was lucky to be in a position to leave my job, go on vacation for two weeks, come back and then go away again for a further three months, if only they knew the truth.

I was booked to fly into New York, not my favourite place but each time I tried to sort out my accommodation, it felt like someone or something was blocking me. A similar thing had happened when I tried to plan my itinerary for the three-month trip. I had a cousin working in New York but being a builder, he was sleeping on the job and that was no place for a lady. Naturally, I was concerned about my living arrangements but every minute spent in London breathed disobedience. The only way to find peace was to be in God's will, so I arranged for my cousin to collect me from JFK airport and planned on figuring the rest out later.

On the morning of my departure I spoke with a friend and informed him of my accommodation status. The only thing that held me together was God's peace but nothing made sense anymore and arriving in New York with no place to lay my head, was the least of my concerns. God had made it clear that I had to go, so I was going.

I arrived at Heathrow Airport and sat chatting with a friend acting like all was well, and all was well because strangely enough, walking into the unknown and trusting in a God I could not see, was the safest place I had been in, in a long time. I did not know it at the time but as I walked in faith and the security that I was feeling, God through His presence was guiding my steps. About an hour before I went through security, I received a call from the friend I had spoken with earlier, who informed me that he had found me somewhere to stay. A friend of his, with whom I was vaguely acquainted but had not seen in almost eighteen years, was willing to put me up. Usually something like that would have had my insecurities and paranoia screaming for cover but instead I was composed, almost as if I had been expecting the news. The calm night flight gave me time to reflect on the past few months but the realisation of what I was doing had not yet registered. When I arrived in New York at Pam's house I was nervous. I did not do the whole "I'm a friend of a friend, can I stay at your house?" thing but she and her husband were very welcoming and their warmness stilled the handful of fears that were trying to get my attention.

I was out of my comfort zone yet I was comfortable.

It was evident this was where I was supposed to be. Pam was astounded by my faith and spoke of how I served as an encouragement to her. I had not given my movements any thought, I just wanted to be at peace and following God's instructions brought me peace. She pointed out that when she heard I was at the airport about to get on a plane with no idea where I was going to stay, she saw that as a step of faith and wanted to meet the person who was bold enough to take such a step. She saw me as being bold, all I saw was an anxious young woman, who had left all she knew and had no idea of where she was going, or what she was doing.

# 3

# A New Dawn

I think it is fair to say, I had no problems recognising God's voice but recognising His voice did not quieten the other voices that encouraged me to dwell on my past. After a shaky start, it seemed God was tired of my pity party and was ready to get things rolling. I spent two weeks at Pam's house, mostly in bed thinking about what I had walked away from, what I was going to do and how it was going to happen. I had good days filled with hope and confidence, followed by dark days filled with unpleasant memories that stemmed from my childhood, the death of my mother and life in general. Left to me, I could have spent the next three months there in the basement apartment feeling sorry for myself but God had not sent His best angels to escort me to New York so I could spend my days crying, sleeping and feeling sorry for myself. He had invested in me and He was going to accomplish what He had set out to do! Isaiah knew this to be true of God when God spoke these words through him *"so is my word that goes out from my mouth: It will not return to me empty, but will accomplish what I desire and achieve the purpose for which I sent it."* (Isa 55:11 NIV). Now I knew it too.

When God moves, He chooses how much He wants to reveal and my revelations came step by step. Solomon also knew what I was just finding out, when he recorded *"in their hearts humans plan their course, but the Lord establishes their steps."* (Prov 16:9 NIV). When I left London, all I knew was that I was flying to New York but within the three months I travelled from New York, to Orlando, Atlanta, Virginia, South Carolina, Dallas and Palm Springs.

My introverted nature got the shock of its life as God pushed me completely out of my comfort zone, causing me to have to speak and interact with strangers and accept their help. I was a giver not a receiver but God wanted me to be a giver *and* a receiver. I had to accept the help of others in order to survive and God used people to bless me financially, provide accommodation, transportation and support. He led strangers to purchase plane tickets for me, people gave up their beds for me and almost everyone I came into contact with had a word for me.

I like to keep to myself; I would sooner walk away before I ask for help and have others think of me as being incompetent but on this trip, I had to open my mouth and speak. I had to learn to say "yes please" and "thank you," and every time I accepted help, my flesh felt like it was dying a painful death. To say God provided would not do justice to Him; He exceeded all my expectations. He certainly did do *"immeasurably more than all we ask or imagine"* (Eph 3:20 NIV) and each time He moved, I was humbled. I learned the value of spending quality time with Him and missed Him tremendously when I was otherwise engaged; I was falling in love with Him and I mean really falling in love with Him.

I had been a Christian for many years but this trip was my first major encounter with the true and living God. By that I mean, instead of reading about Him and trying to understand Him with my head knowledge, I was now reading, encountering and communicating with Him through my spirit, causing Him to become real and our encounters intimately personal.

One of the most profound, life changing moments on the trip came about on the last night of a conference I was attending. Left to me, I would not have been there in the first place because I do not 'do' crowds but it was *not* up to me.

Where God led. I simply followed. Earlier that day, He had informed me I had to tell my story. 'Story' I thought, what story did I have to tell and who would be interested? The thought of documenting my life on paper for all to see, was not met with my approval. Firstly, nothing in my life was worth reading about and secondly, some things from my past needed to be left there! Truthfully, I was scared and I remember pleading with God and asking Him if I could wait until my father was dead, as I felt certain things that had happened might not sit well with others and I wanted to protect him. However, God was adamant and firm in His answer. *"No!"* He said *"it is not about you; it's about what I have done for you and what I am going to do through you."* So, I wrote down everything He told me and pondered on it throughout the day.

As the conference drew to a close, I sat in my chair praying and reflecting, when immediately the auditorium became silent and empty and I saw myself sitting on a chair in the centre of the arena with a spotlight on me. As I sat with my head bowed low a voice spoke.

*"It was never about you."*

"What was never about me?" I replied.

*"Everything that happened to you, it was never about you."*

I sat in silence listening with my heart, mind and spirit. Of late, visions like this had become a normal part of day to day living and drew me closer to God and I had no reason to doubt it was God because I had read of similar occurrences in the bible.

*"You think I just decided to use you but you were created for this purpose and all the negative things that happened to you, happened to steer you away from this purpose."*

I remained silent and somewhat bewildered by the information and the fact that the voice had read the thoughts that had been plaguing my mind from the time

God told me to leave my job. I was convinced God woke up one day and just decided He wanted to use me, which in itself is ridiculous because God never sleeps. It never occurred to me that I had been called all along and why would it? My childhood had been tarnished with damaging verbal and physical abuse. I had lost my mum in my mid teens and her death had caused more personal problems. I had built an unstable lifestyle based on negative thoughts and I had repeatedly done many things the bible said I should not do. I loved God and I wanted and needed His love but He could not use me, He just couldn't.

"So, it was not my fault? I was not a bad evil child?"

*"Everything that happened to you was instigated by the enemy to keep you bound; it is not about you, it is not about what is inside you. He is trying to kill what's inside you."*

The auditorium was still silent and I was still sitting on the chair, head bowed. I felt like someone was running through my body switching on all the lights, answering all the questions I had never voiced. It was liberating and as the truth hit home, tears began to flow and I was back in my setting, back in the conference with thousands of people around me.

I sat for a while slightly dazed by God's Words but silently overjoyed and in awe that He was ministering to me the way He was. Everything He did made perfect sense in the

Spirit but could not be comprehended in the flesh. It was a lot to take in. God loved me and was speaking to me in ways I had only read of. He had chosen me before I was born to do what He was now calling me to do; Paul was aware of this but I was yet to fully grasp that *"Even before he made the world, God loved us and chose us in Christ to be holy and without fault in his eyes. God decided in advance to adopt us into his own family by bringing us to himself through Jesus Christ. This is what he wanted to do, and it gave him great pleasure. So we praise God for the glorious grace he has poured out on us who belong to his dear Son. — Furthermore, because we are united with Christ, we have received an inheritance from God, for he chose us in advance, and he makes everything workout according to his plan."* (Eph 1: 4–6, 11 NIT)

God had placed something inside me, something Paul understood when he wrote *"For we are God's handiwork, created in Christ Jesus to do good works, which God Prepared in advance for us to do."* (Eph 2:10 NIV). This was a threat to the devil and something he wanted to destroy. Peter was most definitely right when he said *"your enemy the devil prowls around like a roaring lion looking for someone to devour."* (1 Pet 5:8 NIV). He is a thief and as John reminds us, *"the thief comes only to steal and kill and destroy; I have come that they may have life, and have it to the full."* (Jn 10:10 NIV) My eyes were opened to this new understanding of my past in such a way it took my breath away. I silently collected my things, exchanged numbers with those I had met and made my way back to where I was staying.

Anytime God did something, it involved movement and growth. Now I had answers, I no longer had excuses.

I was changing. I was stronger and I had a purpose and having a purpose made a difference. I no longer just existed, my life had meaning but most of all my encounters with God were drawing me closer to the God I never really knew and I learned that He had not changed. *"He was the same yesterday, today and forever."* (Heb 13:8 NIV). To be experiencing Him in such dimensions left me hungry for more and exposed me to the depth of His passionate love for me. Who was I that He should treat me this way? I was ordinary, no special qualifications, no deeds to impress. I did not always listen neither was I a model student when it came to obedience. And let's not talk about doubts and fears!

So, what qualified me for such treatment? Like you, I was His child and what He was doing for me is what He desires to do for us all.

Whilst at the conference in Tampa, Florida, I made friends with a group of women who sent me a plane ticket to visit them in Virginia. I remember thinking how awesome God was that He would do such a thing for me, I thought this type of thing only happened to well known ministers of the gospel. During my stay in Virginia, one of the women I was staying with had to go out of town to a funeral but was happy to leave me, a virtual stranger, in her home alone and even stocked the fridge before leaving, so I would not go hungry. As I walked around the house taking in my surroundings, tears of gratitude ran down my cheeks. I was not worthy of what God was doing. I did not know these women and had I not been obedient and spoken to the woman sitting on the grass back in Tampa I would not have been in Virginia and would have missed out on what was happening and what was about to happen. The atmosphere in the house was filled with so much love, the kind that limits your vocabulary. It is so thick you can feel it but you could not explain it. It was evident I had to learn to receive as well as give.

Everything God did, brought me humbly to my knees and later that morning as I was praying, I saw in another vision what looked like an old, dirty piece of 'something or other' laying on the ground. Out of nowhere, a hand picked up the object and placed it inside their coat close to their chest. The next thing I saw was the object sitting on a worktop as the person started chiselling away at what looked like built up old matter. I could not see a body just hands and the object. After a short while, where once sat a dirty looking object, now stood a beautiful, ornate, onyx blue vase. I stared in amazement at the finished product, wondering how something so dirty and disfigured could end up looking so beautiful. The transformation was amazing and the person cleaning it had handled it so lovingly, placing it inside their coat before cleaning it in a way that suggested they knew it's real worth. As I lay prostrate on the floor, my thoughts were interrupted by a voice that said *"This is what I have done with you."* I do not know if I cried more because I never realised how filthy I was, or because God was now saying I was as beautiful as the vase, either way I held my belly and cried and cried. His love was overpowering and His words broke and healed me in the same breath.

The trip lasted three months and by the time I was ready to return home, I had had so many encounters with God I hardly recognised myself but I was confident that everything He had shown me would come to pass and felt it would happen just as I imagined.

I was in a different place and most definitely not the same timid young woman, who months before cowered away in bed hoping the world would disappear and take her with it. I was confident yet humble, happy but nervous, ready to live out what God had shown me but unwilling to wait. I was excited about my future and at times felt like a donkey walking along with a carrot dangling before it, the goal so close but still out of reach. I knew what I wanted and had been fortunate enough to get a small glimpse of what God had planned for me and I wanted it badly.

I was a new person; viewing life through different spectacles.

I would spend hours reading my bible, enjoying God's word and praying. It was like I had the Holy Spirit on tap, steering my every move, pointing out the adjustments I needed to make and correcting me when I wandered off course. I was in love with God and ever grateful for His mercy and love towards me. I was happy and ready to step out and when I spoke, God's words flowed from me, causing me to step back and examine myself. For the first time in my life I spoke confidently about God with my siblings and my father. Although I was a Christian, for me speaking to my family about God had always felt strange and awkward but here I was encouraging them and sharing my testimony.

I shared the conversation I had had with God with my father, explaining how I had wanted to wait until his soul was at rest before I told my story. I informed him of God's view on my stance and to my surprise he gave me his blessing, stating the very words God Himself had used. He said it was not about me; it was about what God was going to do in and through me and went on to say that he was prepared to accept any consequences for his actions. It must have been God himself that picked my jaw up from the floor as I listened in disbelief to the words that were coming out of my father's mouth.

As I made my way home in silence, the constant shaking of my head was the most I could muster to express my views on what had just taken place.

I never doubted God would make things right but I had not expected that kind of response. I expected uproar, followed by distance and finally, reconciliation. It was evident God was in control; all I had to do was to trust and obey Him.

God was faithful and provided me with a part time job that paid a full-time wage, allowing me the time I needed to do His will, whilst enabling me to cover my outgoings and offer help and assistance to others. He brought people into my life with whom I was able to share, encourage and glean wisdom and strength. And it was clear to those who knew me that there had been a change. For the first time in my life, I can truly say I was happy and nothing or no one was going to come between me and God and what I believed.

In time, I started working on my book (A Precious Stone) but not before experiencing major insecurities, as I questioned who would want to read it and did I really have a story to tell?

Once again, I could not deny that God had spoken to me but I saw nothing significant about my life that was worth writing about. I did start writing but the words that came out of my mouth did not line up with my actions. If someone asked me what I was doing with myself, I would reply "I am writing a book, my story but who is going to want to read it?" I never realised at the time but in effect I doubted God and from there on in, things began to change.

Gradually, in ways so minute they were hardly noticeable, I started to drift. I was grateful for God's provision but along the way I got caught up in the job He had provided and the great people I worked with and slowly I started to feel different. I was still covered and protected by God but my time with Him suffered. Some days I would be so guilt-stricken, I would just cry. On other days, I would tell myself God still loved me, I just had to focus and I vowed to do better. I constantly spoke of what I had to do but I was not *doing* it and before I realised it, weeks, months and years ticked by. The more I spoke of what I should have been doing, the worse I felt and questioned why I was not doing it.

The distractions were enormous and the underlining fact was that I did not believe I had a story to tell! Deep down I knew I was disobeying God and more than anything, I wanted to turn things around and go back to how they were when I was tucked away with Him but instead my guilt led me further adrift.

I tried to push past the turmoil inside me and strive for what He had shown me. I continued to smile, suggesting to the outside world all was well but inside I felt like a fraud. I was torn between my love for God, wanting to please Him and my self-imposed insignificance.

# 4

# Who's Your Daddy?

His love is unconditional. He will never leave you or forsake you. Just ask for forgiveness, He is waiting for you. No, He has not changed His mind about you, He still loves you. Of course, your calling still stands. No, you have not missed your chance. God loves you.

If I had a penny for every time I was encouraged or tried to encourage myself, by now I would be a millionaire. Whether I chose to believe it or not, it was true, God had not forgotten me, He had not changed His mind about me and He loved me unconditionally.

He loved the fact that regardless of where I was or what I was thinking, my heart desired to serve Him. I was struggling with obedience but I was humble and I did have a contrite heart. However, that did not mean He approved of my disobedience and somewhat lack of faith in Him. Choosing to dwell on my insecurities meant I placed more emphasis on myself than I did in God. By believing I could not make things happen, I dismissed God from the equation and exposed my lack of faith.

I strongly believe it was my encounters with God whilst away that kept me afloat. Working against my fears, I finally got stuck in and committed to writing my story and as I did, I began to learn a lot about my parents, my siblings and myself. I realised I was responsible for needless blame I had laid at the feet of others and that depression had been a part of my life for so long, it had become my number one spar. If I left it too long to write, I would feel lost and dejected but the minute I got on the computer I felt content and in right standing with God. It was clear, He wanted me to tell my story but it was extremely challenging. Hurts that had ruled my life were being uprooted and laid to rest as truths were exposed and I was able to see where I was wrong and not the victim as I had believed. Even if my story never got published, it was worth writing because it was healing me. I had a few people read some of my work and the general feedback was that I definitely had a story to tell, so God was right, well of course He was right, after all, He is God.

A father knows, or ought to know, his child and God knew me but did I know who God was? Did I know He was my father and wanted nothing but the best for me? Did I know the best did not mean everything would always run smooth but it did mean everything would work out for my good, even the difficulties? Was I ready to hold onto that promise? The one that was so beautifully articulated by Paul, when he wrote *"we know that in all things God works for the good of those who love him, who have been called according to his purpose."* (Rom 8:28 NIV)

I was on a journey that involved me letting go of the person that circumstances and lies had turned me into. I had to rid myself of the person who hoped for nothing and always thought the worst. I had to let go of the person that had so little confidence, she would sooner say she could not do something instead of facing her fear of trying and making a fool of herself, or worse still having to ask for help. In order to be my Father's child, I had to let go — be re-birthed and God seemed to be using my writing to do just that. However, unless I stayed close to Him and remained focused on Him, I was sure to stumble — and stumble I did.

I was back on the roller-coaster of unsettled emotions. One minute I was focused, the next I was being enticed into my surroundings and these surroundings were not conducive to the sensing of God's presence. I was love sick and longed to be back in God's arms locked up in His presence, just the two of us. I wanted God so badly it made me miserable and with misery came the condemnation that I was not good enough.

Of course, you are not good enough, you want God but He does not want you. When was the last time you were whisked away on a vision? When was the last time you heard Him speak? It has been so long, so how can He still love you? The words in my head were never ending, on and on and on. But God did love me; He loved me and was with me even though I could not see it. What I needed to do was lay hold of the truth that *there is now no condemnation for those who are in Christ Jesus.* (Rom 8:1 NIV)

Occasionally when I sensed His presence, I tried to hold onto it for dear life, expecting it to never change but it did. On those days, He could seem distant, almost non-existent, and when that happened, I took it personally. Only God knows what He thought of me, I can see Him now, shaking His head, wondering when I was going to learn that He was my Father and abandoning me was not an option! He promised *"surely I am with you always, to the very end of the age."* (Mt 28:20 NIV)

He was my heavenly Father but I viewed him the same way I viewed my biological father. Growing up, my father had been my hero but he had also been a great disciplinarian and unfortunately, as I got older our relationship did not mirror the father-daughter relationship I had dreamt of. There was so much my father did not know about me, which created distance between us. And despite my previous encounters with God, part of me — a very large part of me — viewed Him in the same way.

What I did not realise was that I was God's child and He knew everything about me. He knew what I was capable of, my likes and dislikes, my dreams and aspirations, my fears and my strengths. He knew that I wanted to please Him and He saw my struggle to separate His personality from that of my biological father. Where I saw chaos, God saw potential and a work-in-progress. Where I saw no hope and no way out, He saw opportunities waiting to be unlocked. When God looked at me, He saw His creation and His creation was a reflection of Himself — I was wonderfully and fearfully made and was capable of doing all things with His help and guidance.

Sometimes when we are experiencing difficulties, God places us in situations where we are required to help others, inadvertently helping ourselves. During these times, if we are willing to lay aside our will for His and trust Him with the mustard seed faith we possess at the present time, we often come away amazed at what He can do with us and through us and how He can use remote situations to answer our prayers and open our eyes. In May 2007, He chose something I would have never dreamed of to remind me of what He had placed in me. To show me how strong I was, how much I had changed and the false identity of my poor self-image. He did this by using me to help draw others closer to Him. Given my present mindset, my assignment should have been enough to make me realise the God whom I claimed to serve, was not only merciful and loving, He was truly God and there was no other beside Him.

Out of the blue, I received a call from a friend who was in trouble and unsure of how to help, I turned to God for direction. Surprisingly, His response was that I should visit her. This was a suggestion that was ridiculous for so many reasons, the main one being she lived in New York and I lived in London. We exchanged words and I finally gave in declaring "if You want me to go, You will have to make a way."

A few days later, I received another call from my friend Pam, in New York. She explained she had a friend she felt I could help and wished I was there to do so in person. I informed her that it was not certain but there was a possibility I was going to be in New York very soon, so it might be possible. No sooner had the phone call ended, I had a strong sense in my spirit that I had to go to New York, which was backed up by a deep sense of peace. After accepting the assignment, it was made clear that part of the trip would involve me flying to Florida to see an old friend, who was under the impression I had not forgiven them, for something they had done a few years prior. The truth was I had forgiven them but they had not forgiven themselves and in doing so were blocking God's love from reaching out to them. I kicked and screamed about going to Florida, complaining to God that it would make me look weak and my friend should come to me because all I ever did was forgive, forgive, forgive.

Word of wisdom: do not ever try to pick an argument with God!

God was calm and patiently waited for me to tire myself out, before pointing out my position with my friend was no different to His position with me, after which I felt rather small and somewhat dim-witted for my outburst.

*"How many times have I told you I've forgiven you for things you've done, only to have you wallow in condemnation because you won't forgive yourself? Then*

*turn around and treat me like I'm holding your sin against you?"*

I was silent.

*"Every time you feel that way I come at you with more and more love because that is who I am and it's the only way I can get you to understand that I love you and hold nothing against you. You say you feel frustrated and hurt because your friend constantly treats you like you have not forgiven them. How do think I feel when you do the same thing to me?"*

What could I say? Like God, all I wanted to do was lavish my friend with kindness and sincerity in the hope that they would see I had forgiven them and there were no hard feelings. However, the more kindness I showed, the more they pulled away out of guilt, unable to accept my forgiveness, love, compassion and loyalty. I was getting a minute taste of what God goes through on a daily basis. Only He does not deal with just one person but most of the human population. It was heart-breaking. Every time I questioned why my friend could not accept my forgiveness, I felt a lump in my throat. The desire to express nothing but love and kindness towards them increased and with it the reality of how I treat God and how He treats me.

The funds rolled in and I booked the five-day trip but I needed instructions of what to do and what to say when I arrived. In need of a plan, I went on a two-week fast, seeking direction from God. I spent the first week cleansing myself, reading and meditating on God's word and by week two felt confident He was going to give me words for each individual I was due to visit. However, when week two arrived, He told me I had to empty myself because on this trip, I was to be the vessel and He was going to work through me.

The two people I had planned to see in New York were expecting me but I was a little concerned that visiting my friend in Florida would be a waste of time, as they had no idea of my visit, neither were they accepting my calls. In an attempt to help the situation, I questioned God, who made it clear I was not to contact them. Surprised, I asked Him what was the point of going if they did not know I was coming? How could I be certain they would be there and what was I supposed to do when I got there? Showing me a pair of yellow marigold gloves, God's response was ***"I want you to clean the house."***

Uh? Clean the house! Was this some kind of joke? Surely, I had not heard right?

"You want me to go all the way to Florida to clean someone's house? That's ludicrous!"

Fasting and being in His presence made it almost impossible to argue. So in obedience, I went to the shop, purchased some gloves and Ajax cleaner, packed my bags and set off for the States.

In New York, I took a back seat, as I watched God work through me to help and bless others. I opened my mouth and He spoke. His words to the individuals were loving and firm but amongst them were warnings of aspects in their lives that needed to change. He had flown me all the way from London to minister to them because they were important to Him. God loved them so much, He was willing to do whatever it took to show them. I remember thinking if only He did something like that for me I would be blown away but He had done that and more and I still doubted Him.

Upon leaving New York, I flew to Florida, where my real test of faith in God would be tried and with my stomach in knots, I drove from the airport to my friend's house.

Was I nervous? I had not seen them in over three years and was about to turn up on their doorstep unannounced with instructions from God to clean their house. Of course, I was nervous! I was so nervous, I spent an hour or so outside, a few streets away, texting my Pastor and flatmate back in London informing them I was too scared to knock on the door.

What if they were not receptive of my presence? What if they did not open the door? What if this was a big mistake? Why would God send me overseas just to clean someone's house? As for the marigold gloves, it must have been hunger playing tricks on me! Such were the thoughts running through my mind, and attached to them was a deep sense of fear. As fearful as I felt and as stupid as it seemed, I had come thus far leaning on God and I could not turn back now.

As I drove up the driveway and parked the car, I knew I could not turn back, even if I wanted to. Once they heard the car, they would be sure to be peering through the window. They would see me before I saw them.

What would they think?

Concentrating to put one foot in front the other whilst holding my breath, I made my way to the front door and knocked. Seconds later came a voice asking "who is it?" "It's Jemma" I replied. Stomach churning and uncertain of what to expect, I braced myself for our first meeting since the incident three years ago. I am not sure what was going through their head but there was silence and the door remained closed.

"Ok, I didn't expect this, now what?" If I did not feel like an idiot before, I certainly felt like one now! I wanted to turn around, head back to my car and get out of there as fast as my legs would carry me but I could not move.

After a while, I heard the door unlock and a shocked friend stood before me. As it turned out my fears had been for nothing because they were happy to see me, shocked — but happy — and they proceeded to invite me in. There was no awkward silence, just a huge grin on their face.

Walking past them, I wondered how I would break the news of the reason for my visit and tried to take in the surroundings I had been instructed to clean. The blinds were closed and the house was dark, so I could not see much but what little I could see, seemed ok. Once we had got the casual greetings out the way, I explained the reason for my visit. I thought they would be confused by my news but instead they handed me the keys to the house (almost like they were expecting me) and we agreed I would return the following morning when the house was empty, to commence my task.

I spent most of that evening in a daze, trying to take in what had happened. Not only had my friend given me the keys, they did not think it strange that I had come all the way from London to clean their house. In fact, they accompanied me to the store to get more cleaning stuff!

The following morning after everyone had left, I returned to the house, opened the door and as daylight exposed the inside, the scene that greeted me left me astounded. All I can say is when God said clean the house, He meant clean the house! Unable to move, I paused in awe of the God some say does not exist or never speaks to them and marvelled at His greatness.

He had given me explicit instructions, which all along I thought were ridiculous but He had seen what needed to be done. He had sent help.

I was in shock. Not so much at the state of the house but the fact that I had been praying back home in London, when God showed me a pair of gloves and told me to go to Florida to clean a house that truly needed cleaning. I could not get past the fact that His instructions were so on point! That even though I recognised His voice and was one hundred percent certain that I had not been mistaken, I had questioned Him but beyond that, the house really, really needed cleaning. Mouth ajar, l looked on in disbelief, any moment expecting something to run across the room. I was scared, not of the task in hand but of what may be hiding beneath all the mess and chaos. When I finally came to my senses, I wondered how my friend could be happy living this way and then wondered where to start. To be honest, I felt the mission was far more than I could handle and it pushed me to my limits but I kept reminding myself that God had said to clean the house and I assure you, He was not joking when He showed me those gloves, as boy did I need them.

Confident in areas I would have otherwise been squeamish, I set to work cleaning as if it were my own home and was amazed at the love I felt as I did so. This was not me, I did not function this way and I did not do grime! Yet I was humbled and felt myself ceasing to be, as God worked through me.

It truly was an amazing experience.

I excelled above my limitations by trusting God and taking Him at His word, as opposed to relying on my own understanding. During the task I was determined, alert and undeterred. It was an emotional time because so much love went into the cleaning; you could feel it in the atmosphere. The love that was displayed came from so deep within, I never knew I had such depth and the willingness to please would have had me on the roof if necessary. In the afternoon, when my friend returned from work, they joined me in the clean, getting stuck in as passionately as I was and admitted they knew the house needed cleaning but just did not know where to start. They had become so overwhelmed by their surroundings, they were being sucked in, and they did not know where to turn for help. As we continued to clean, neither of us spoke and by the time we were finished, it looked like a completely different house, homely and liveable.

At the end of the day, God's message to my friend was simple and clear but it was not until we were done that He began to show me the connection. The house was a representation of their life and just as the house needed cleaning up, so too did their life. God wanted them to know He loved them and had chosen to do things this way, so that they would not be mistaken about His love for them. He also wanted them to know that I had forgiven them but was only able to do so because of His love flowing through me. It was all about God. If I had not forgiven them, it would have been impossible for me to humble myself enough to do what I did and with such love. We both learned a lot that day and little by little, I could see why God had chosen to do things the way He had. If He did not, Mark would have gone on believing that I had not forgiven him for the breakup and may have continued to live in condemnation over what had happened. This way, he had no choice but to accept that I had forgiven him, that God loved him and wanted Him to sort out his life. That He had taken care of me and now wanted to do the same for him. As for me, He wanted me to know Him more through the experience.

After bidding my friend goodbye and encouraging him to put God's word into action, I went back to my hotel and whatever had been carrying me left and a deep tiredness took over. Laying in bed, exhausted, I tried to take in the events of the past few days. It was like I had been present but only watching from the outskirts. What exactly had just happened?

Waiting at the airport to board my flight home I had time to reflect on what I had seen and what God had done through me. He had shown me that He sees and knows everything, that without Him I could do nothing but with Him all things were possible. Nothing about the trip was coincidental and following His instructions, regardless of how crazy they seemed, had caused me to see first-hand what He was capable of and proved He is the all-seeing, all-knowing God.

# 5

# The Danger of Barely Existing

After such an experience, I should have been enjoying the scenes from the top of the mountain but within days I was wallowing in the despair of the valley. I felt so low, it was hard to believe that I had accompanied God on such a mission. It was as if I had come out of the supernatural and into the natural and the natural had nothing to offer. For days I questioned God on why I was feeling the way I was and why I was so tired but He was silent. I now believe He was silent because I should have taken time to rest in Him and allow Him to minister to me, instead of just opting to live off the memory of my assignment and needless to say it was not long before depression set in.

It's ok, you can ask. "How could I end up depressed after such an experience?" I asked myself the same question and came up with same answer. I did not allow God to complete what He had started and to reveal what He wanted me to get from the assignment. I should have taken time out to rest in Him, to seek Him, allowing Him to minister to me as I had prior to commencing the trip but I did not. I saw it as Him wanting to help others but never stopped long enough for Him to reveal all of what He wanted to reveal to me, for me and about me. I was incomplete because I was absent without leave.

I tried to hold onto the memory of the trip and feed off it. I told myself I was called by God and more assignments like it would follow but they did not. I criticised myself for not being able to hold onto God's gaze and in time, welcomed the enemy's arguments, that once again I had failed to please my Father. Regardless of how I tried, I could not get back up and believe me I tried. I enrolled in bible school. I studied. I prayed. I continued my writing. Ok... I struggled with my writing but I was still writing. I was still attending church and more than ever, helping others and putting them before myself but inside, little by little, I was ceasing to exist.

Time was slipping by and before I knew it weeks and months had turned into years. What was I doing? Where was I going? By the time I caught myself and cried out to others for help, I had become a victim of my own success because everyone thought I was strong enough to pull through. I tried crying out to God but He was not answering me like He used to. So, I naturally drew the conclusion that I was a disappointment to Him, again! I still believed in Him but I doubted He still believed in me. I was doing to Him, what had been done to me. I was throwing His love, compassion and forgiveness back in His face because I could not forgive myself for not being as committed to Him as I desired to be. All of His teachings and my experiences with Him went out the window, as I chose to focus on the negative evidence, as opposed to the unseen truth.

In early 2008, I began a slow spiral into a depression that lasted the best part of three years, with me periodically popping up for air. I threw myself into projects that allowed me to forget about myself and concentrate on helping others. I disliked being so busy but being busy kept my thoughts at bay. If I was not volunteering my services at church, I was fundraising to assist my charity work abroad. I even enrolled in a twelve month 'Christian Counselling Skills' course, in the hope that along the way I would receive revelation of my calling. Keeping busy was necessary for my survival and helped mask the depression but I felt lost. I looked for things I was good at and hoped God would give His nod of approval, an indication that I was on the right path. I desperately craved His intimate attention but gained nothing. I set deadlines to complete my book, thinking that would be the key to my release. But the book was a huge task that could not be rushed and all I wanted to do was finish it and get it out of the way. I spoke with ministers from my church and close friends but nothing was helping. Nothing anyone did or said filled the void for the intimacy my inner being craved.

By 2010, I had digressed so much that I struggled to face each day. Over time, I had merged into a solidified state of barely existing and what little energy I had was used to prop myself up to face the world with my fake smile. "I'm ok. I'm fine. I'm as well as can be expected." Press the play button and let the role play begin. They dare not see what is really going on; if they do, I will be labelled a failure. Do they know I am here? Do they see my pain, and more to the point would they miss me if I were not here? Such were the daily conversations with myself.

My mind became a theatre as I played back scenes from my past, meditating on the lows and cancelling out the highs and the more I watched the scenes, the deeper I sunk. By summer 2010, I had sunk so low I hardly attended church and just about forced myself to go to work for the two days a week I was employed. When I was not working, daily tasks such as brushing my teeth, having a wash and eating, were a struggle that used up all my will power. All I wanted to do was close my eyes and kiss the world goodbye.

I was so desperate I was beginning to scare myself.

My prayer life was stale and intimacy with God was a fantasy. More than ever, I was hungry for Him and my desire for Him tormented me. Would I ever find Him and be free in Him as I had been before? What about the visions, revelations and words He had poured into me? What had I done with them and where had they gone? I had opted to doubt God's word over my life and now without it, I was wandering in the wilderness in search of it. It felt like I had the weight of the world on my shoulders. I was lonely and scared and if I could not connect with God, I had nothing.

It never occurred to me to take time out and I cannot for the life of me understand why, especially after my last trip. That should have been my first port of call but instead I hoped that I could get on my knees, call out to God and immediately be back at the place I had been before. Writing this, I now realise I was not prepared to pay the cost to get back what I had lost because I was not truly aware of what I had lost. For the longest time I felt God had let me down by not quenching my hunger for Him, so He was responsible for my predicament, and if He was responsible and was not doing anything about it, what hope did I have? It seemed the only release from my torment was death.

Very few people knew how low I had become and I liked it that way because it meant I did not have to answer to anyone. I wanted 'out' but I did not have the energy to get out. I was tired, tired of returning to the same stumbling block and falling at the same hurdle. This time if I made it out, there was no way I could return, I was like a dog returning to its vomit and I had returned one too many times. Something had to give but what? I periodically confessed that my breakthrough was so overdue, it stunk and that is how it felt, like it was there on my doorstep waiting for me and was now past its due date. Often it felt like Satan himself had my stuff in the palm of his hand and all I had to do was take it. But however hard I tried, I could not get it back. If wanting it back with all my heart, mind and soul was not enough, then what was? If praying, crying and reaching out to God over and over and over again was not enough, then what was? If lying in bed desperate, scared, emotional and lonely was not enough to get God's attention, then what was? What did I have to do for God to realise I had come to the end of my tether and needed His help?

Over time, I began to understand why people left home and never returned, disappearing without a trace. Why some walked the streets talking to themselves, until eventually they were labelled crazy and why others opted to end the torment, by taking their own lives. Without ceasing, the words in my head were like quicksand, dragging me down to their level, allowing me no time to reason.

All along I had had my own ideas about how God's plan was going to come to pass and I believe that trying to interject my concept into His will is what caused me to find myself back at ground zero — depressed, invisible, lost and feeling like a continual disappointment. The truth was, all along God longed for me to come home but like the prodigal son, I too felt like I had to get myself together before I could face Him. How would I do that, when He was the only one who could make me whole and bring me back to where I needed to be?

Until now, I had never likened myself to the prodigal son but that is precisely whose shoes I was wearing. Eating food thrown to pigs and scrambling around in the darkness, while all the time there was a safe house and a loving father waiting, longing to see me approaching from a distance. He wanted His child home safe, where He could watch over me, cover and protect me. To see me going astray hurt God more than I realised. I was part of Him. How could He rest until I was back home with Him where I belonged? Now I understand the love of the father. Now I understand the mindset of the prodigal son; what kept him in a state of nothingness and what caused him to return home.

Like the prodigal son, one minute I was in the sty unable to face my Father, the next I had purposed in my mind that I had to find Him. Death was still knocking at my door, in fact death had stepped up its game but something within needed and craved the gaze of God my Father and I had to go to Him. I was not in search of a change or a breakthrough; I was in search of life, the bread of life that came direct from God. Life that would destroy every deep rooted stronghold, lie, deception and negative experience the enemy had fed me. At aged forty-one, I had battled and debated with him for long enough. His lies and all traces of my life that centred on them, had to be destroyed because I wanted to be set free and be free indeed. Whatever it took I was going to do it. I wanted and needed to establish new habits; Godly habits that would become a part of me and hold me secure through life's storms, without me having to stumble at the same hurdle ever again. I was as desperate to live as I had been to die and there could be only one winner.

Life or death?

# 6

# The Return

Choosing life meant that every part of me that was linked to my depressive triggers had to be destroyed. Choosing life meant a completely new start. Not some 'self-help away break' or a stint of counselling. I had been there, done that. Choosing life meant living life; experiencing the reality of my desires; being re-birthed. This was going to be a new start, with no way of returning to one's old self. Could I be confident in God's promise that, *"He who began a good work in you will carry it on to completion until the day of Christ Jesus?"* (Phil 1:6 NIV)

It was returning to one's old self that had always fuelled my depression. Here we go again, when is it going to end? I was overwhelmed by drained emotions, fatigue, tears, heaviness, loss, darkness, pity and more. All these negative elements were killing me from the inside out.

I had experienced God enough to know that in Him there was a peace and joy that nothing or no one but He could bestow. Nothing in the world and nothing I could dream of compared to it. His joy, peace and contentment made everything alright and could make the most painful journey seem like a walk in the park. His peace burrowed deep down, creating a stillness that was humanly impossible and more precious than life itself. It made life worth living. If I could experience Him in my daily life and be confident in Him as He was in me, then I could beat this thing once and for all. If I could create new habits, that caused everything I said and did to be God centred, then I could walk through the valley of the shadow of death and truly fear no evil. My desire fuelled me just enough energy to push past the doubts and reach for what I believed was my last chance of survival.

I needed time away with no distractions. I needed time away with no one but God and myself present. I needed to find God, speak with Him, listen to Him and most importantly, to obey Him. I needed to find a reason for going on. A reason for believing that did not just come from the pulpit but from an assurance within, that God was with me, that He loved me and I was going to make it. I needed to invest in my personal relationship with God and make it a priority in my life. I needed to answer the question — how important was God to me and what value did I place on the role He wanted to play in my life?

Memories of my last trip flooded my mind and the more I dwelled on them, the more appealing my time away became. I had a lot to bring to the table. Aside from my spiritual status, there were everyday issues that needed addressing but I could not just blurt them out to God and demand answers. Yes, they were important but so was my spiritual life. If I was going to make any form of progress, my approach had to be humble and my priorities had to be in order.

Whilst under the belief that I had planned my upcoming trip and it had nothing whatsoever to do with the Holy Spirit or God ordering my steps, it was my intention to take time out to spend with God and pick up from where we had left off in 2005. I had an agenda which was mainly to spend time in prayer and I believed God would show-up purely on the basis that I had taken time out to be with Him. This was my sacrifice and He would honour it.

Judging from my last trip, we were going to have a whirlwind love connection that would hold me secure and I was going to be swept away by Him. Aside from the spiritual aspect of things during our time together, I was going to pray about my book, moving house, (should I buy or rent?), ministry, living abroad and marriage. These were things that the enemy was using to fuel my depression, so naturally they were part of my agenda and because they were my desires, I believed it was part of God's agenda too. I generally do not move without seeking Him first and I needed His opinion and guidance on all of the above.

About six weeks before my trip, I decided to go on a fast and felt the longer the fast, the better the results. I was so desperate to make it right with God, I was willing to try anything. I cannot even remember how I stumbled upon the 'Daniel fast' but after some research, although it was different to the fasts I was accustomed to, I felt it was the right move for me. The 'Daniel fast' lasted for twenty-one days and I planned it so it finished the day before I departed. I was going to use it as preparation for the trip, so that when I arrived, I would be in the right frame of mind. The fast prohibited me eating meat or fish, dairy products, sweeteners, leavened breads and yeast goods. Refined and processed foods, deep-fried foods, solid fats and any beverage other than distilled, filtered or spring water and freshly squeezed juices were not allowed. My diet was made up of fruits, vegetables, nuts and seeds, unleavened breads, no sugars or preservatives. Legumes, good quality oils, such as olive, coconut and grapeseed, fresh herbs, spices, tofu and soy products.

The fast meant I had to be disciplined in what I ate and I used a book, which accompanied the fast, following its daily guide of devotionals and scripture readings.

To go from struggling, to connect with God, to now making Him a priority, meant that my daily schedule worked around Him instead of the other way around. I knew I had to reinstall new habits and this was the best place to start my intimate love relationship with God my number one priority.

By week three, I made sure nothing interrupted my time with God and I realised I was a lot calmer and settled within myself. Still under the belief the decision to go on the fast was my idea, I thought at some point I would be able to incorporate my prayer list but the fast took on a direction of its own and my list never came up in conversation. Instead, I was exposed to the distance that had developed between God and myself, whilst still experiencing His love. I had planned to take two months out of my schedule to spend time with God and the thought of continuing my journey with Him behind closed doors, with no distractions, excited me. As I spent time in my study, I further learned that everything I was about to encounter was God's initiative, God's will, God's purpose and God's plan.

Every bright idea I took credit for was entirely down to God!

Everything as I knew it was about to change. Just as my approach to the trip had been different, so my experiences would be different also. If I had had the slightest inkling of what I was about to experience, I would probably have ran away from God, on the basis that I was not worthy. If this was how He treated me when I was out of His will, then how much more when I was slam bang in the middle of it?

I knew I was changing but I had been here before and did not want to get too excited about my progress because like before, I had also lost my way and ended up at the same stumbling block. But deep down, I knew this time was different, for reasons only God and myself were aware of. As my time for departure drew near I was stilled, calm and ready to spend my days in His presence. I had purposed to spend at least eight hours a day with God, utilising the time to read, pray and write and I admit there was an amount of uncertainty about how He was going to manifest Himself but based on my last trip, I had a few pre-conceived ideas.

When I laid my head to rest on Friday March 11th 2011, I awoke on Saturday 12th right where God wanted me. Unbeknown to me, I had completed twenty-one days of consecration, which had enabled Him to bring me to a place where I could listen, as He spoke and directed my steps. This was my trip that He had planned for me and what a trip it would be!

*The Lord is my Shepheard*
*I shall not want*
*He makes me lie down in green pastures*
*He leads me besides still waters*
*He restores my soul*

PSALM 23:1-3 ESV

# 7

# An Invitation of Love

As I boarded the plane and made myself comfortable in my seat, I found myself reflecting on the last twenty-one days. It felt as if I had gone from being a stranger to God, to His beloved daughter. I was calm in spirit, more relaxed and looked forward to two months of uninterrupted time alone with God. Headed for New York, I was unsure of how long I would be there but purposed to leave it in God's hands.

I was at peace.

I knew I had made progress in the last twenty-one days but I was not looking for progress, I was looking for change, permanent change. I was looking forward to intimacy with God and answered prayers. I was looking forward to Him taking control, going above and beyond what I can think or desire. I was looking forward to asking and being answered, seeking and finding, knocking and having the doors opened wide enough for me to run through them and into the centre of God's heart.

If I had to describe how I felt inside, the word I would use would be 'free'. I was free from the mundane daily rituals;

no calls, no concerns, no worries, no work and no chores. Before me lay an open door, a rare opportunity; I could either use it or abuse it and as I chose to make full use of it, I was reminded that not many of us get a chance like this.

I thought of the married woman who longs to steal away to Father's arms but has a duty to her husband. I thought of the mother who dreams of a break, some peace and quiet to read, study and absorb the word but the children need tending to and when that is done there it is the housework, followed by tomorrow's issues, not to mention her duty to her husband. I thought of the husband who yearns to fulfil the pulling in his heart for more of Father but upon him lies the responsibility of being the breadwinner, the head of his home. The father, who loves his children but with the addition of each child comes the responsibility to provide for them, and as that load increases, time with Father decreases, while the desire and dream to be alone with Him intensifies.

So yes, I was blessed and privileged to be here, who would not want to spend uninterrupted time alone with God?

My first few days were peaceful, just what I need, I felt like I was resting in His arms. I spent time reading the bible and whilst continuing my study on 'Experiencing God', I learnt to let go of my agenda. There was a still calmness in the air that seemed to be dominating my behaviour. It was not something I was used to, yet seemed rather familiar. I was happy — more than happy — and confident in the unknown. Through my studies, I also learned that God initiates and invites; He makes the first move. He draws us to Himself and I sensed that was what this time away was all about. I thought He opened all the doors for me to travel because I longed for time alone with Him and making a way was confirmation I was on the right road but I was wrong. God planned it and invited me. I said yes, and without realising it, made the necessary adjustment to follow and obey. It has little to do with our desire for Him but more about His desires for you and me.

Sometimes we place too much emphasis on ourselves and forget that God is our creator and the creator of the universe we live in. Nothing happens without His knowledge and anything that draws us closer to Him is a direct result of His involvement.

In New York, I stayed with my friend Pam, the same woman who took me in on my last trip. I had my own space and I knew Pam and her husband would not be put off by me excluding myself from their presence. By now they knew me well enough to recognise that if I was there behind closed doors, then God was in control.

One thing I have learned about being alone with God, is that when He speaks, He can say the simplest of things, possibly something you already know. When He speaks, it opens up something inside of you that illuminates your entire being, cleansing the darkest of places.

After allowing me time over the weekend to settle in, come Monday morning, God was ready to get started. His first lesson to me was about love. Personally, I felt I knew all there was to know about God's love for me but it seems at times I made it more complicated than it needed to be. If His love for me was so simple, why was it so hard to comprehend?

Lesson number one...

God wants me! He wants me because He loves me. He went to all this trouble to pull me away to be with Him because He loves me. He blessed me and opened doors that enabled me to come away with Him because I am so important to Him, He cannot bear to lose me. I am important to Him because He loves me and everything He has done and is doing is a result of His love and affection for me.

God loves us; you must know and believe that God loves you.

This is a simple revelation with so much depth. Easy to say, hear and read, yet powerfully thought provoking. Simple words that reduce me to tears, as I come to realise I had not fully grasped the powerful simplicity of His unconditional love for me. Everything God does to keep us close to Him, stems from the depth of His love for us. The bible says He is a jealous God but until now it never occurred to me that His jealousy stemmed from His love and not just His anger. God does not want anything in our lives to receive more attention than Him because He wants nothing but the best for us. As we bestow our affections on Him, He is free to direct our path, protect us and pour out His endless affections upon us. God sent His son Jesus to die for us because His heart was pining with love for us. Jesus obeyed first, out of His love for His father and second out of His love for us. That right there is a whole lot of love!

So, there I was, not picking up from where we had left off in 2005, not even thinking or talking about my prayer list and numerous requests. I was there being taught by God about why I was there. I was there because He loves me and He wanted me to accept what He is saying to me and adjust my thinking and lifestyle to match up with what He is saying. I needed to adjust my thinking and lifestyle to the fact that God loves me.

The reason He was revealing His love to me was because I often gauge it from a human perspective, one with conditions. Now He was showing me, not only did He die for me while I was still a sinner, in the midst of my disobedience and wandering over the last six years, He had pulled me away from everything and it was He who had planned this two month vacation away from everything so that He could expose me to His love and the great value He placed on my life.

Little by little it was sinking in. This trip was not about God directing me to the right publisher for my book, what aspects of ministry He wanted me to go into, whether I should buy a house or rent, or finding a partner. This trip was God's romantic getaway that He planned for me to express how much He loved me.

It was up to me to adjust my way of thinking and adapt to His truths about me. It was up to me to adjust my steps so that I walked in His truth and obeyed whatever instructions He gave me. It was up to me to wait on Him and let Him take the lead because this was not my getaway, it was His. The schedule was set by Him and every directive He gave me was centred on adjustments I need to make in my thinking and lifestyle in order to come into alignment with His Words over me. Then when He felt I was ready, all the other things I was bringing to the table would be addressed.

The desire I had for intimacy with Him was not my desire as previously thought but rather His. He desired to be intimate with me, so that I could know Him through the experience. God loves us far more than we could ever love Him and without His Spirit in us, it is impossible for us to know love, for God is love and it is His Spirit that wills us to do all things.

His word for me was — He loves me and the scriptures He used were like kisses from heaven.

# 8

# Kisses from the Lord

I have been locked away with God for ten days now and He is most definitely the focus of my daily routine. I am fully aware it would be impossible to have this amount of contact with Him were I at home; therefore it is vital I make the most of this opportunity and find myself absorbing every minute detail He has undertaken.

We cannot waste God's time!

My studies and my time with Him, highlight the fact that the most important thing in my life should be my personal intimate love relationship with God and I find my mindset adjusting to this belief. As well as this being the most important thing in my life, it is also the most important part of God's relationship with me. More than anything, He desires intimacy with us and this revelation caused my heart to be more receptive to His love. As I meditated on His love for me, from His perspective and as I read His Word, everything became personal.

*"I have loved you my people (Jemma) with an everlasting love. With an unfailing love I have drawn you to myself. I*

*will rebuild you virgin Israel (Jemma). You will be happy and dance merrily with your tambourines."* (Jer 31:3–4 NLT)

Whilst reading and meditating on the above scripture, tears flowed down my cheeks as I began to realise that God truly does love me and I mean *really* loves me as an individual. I know I have mentioned this before but the realisation of where God's jealousy stems from, is truly amazing. He is jealous because He loves us and does not want to share us with anything or anyone. How did I not see this before?

As more of His revelations were made clear, a sense of love filled the room, unlocking blocked mind-sets and revealing more truths of His love. He was calm and He was with me. I sensed Him sitting beside me. His presence still, warm and overpowering, caused me to become totally transparent before Him with no shame of what was revealed. The truth of my trip and the love behind it, hit home.

He had instigated this time away out of His love for me, whilst I had been unfaithful and He was making me right with Himself because He did not want to lose me, because He loves me.

His love is so deep it draws you closer, leaving you hungry. You want it, you need it and will do anything to hold onto it's grasp.

As I sat reflecting on what He was showing me, the love of my Father became very real. His love is so pure and innocent, it blocks out all doubts. It is so deep, it can rescue you from anything. In silence, more uncontrollable tears flowed, as I began to give in to His love and in return released my gratitude.

*Thank you Father for not giving up on me but for drawing me close to You, behind closed doors. For loving me so much that You would pull me away to be alone with You. Oh how You love me. I never realised how much I meant to You, how important I am to You. You are leading me into an intimate love relationship with You and like a true lover, You have taken care of all the details. I have nothing to concern myself with other than giving myself to You. Take me and break me, I am nothing without You, I am ready to receive all You will have me do, Your way and Your way alone! Forgive me for hurting You. Oh how You love me. You have loved me with an everlasting, unfailing love. Father thank you for my songs and Your kiss.*

*With love from your daughter.*

Sweet Holy Spirit enter my chamber
Speak to me softly as I close the door
Heavenly lover let your presence hover
Shekhinah unending is what I long for

— DAVID INGLES —

# 9

# A Heart to Heart with God

This morning as I opened my eyes, a smile came over my face at the thought of meeting with God. My day began with quiet prayer and praise followed by reading His Word. After an hour or so, I broke for breakfast, exercise and a shower before resuming my studies. It was not how I would normally begin my day, as exercise was not part of my daily routine but on this getaway, God was taking care of the spiritual, while I took care of the physical and a good exercise routine sets you well on your way for the day!

I was fully aware that when I returned home, my days would be very different but whilst away I wanted to make the most of everything accessible to me. I was not just spending time with God, I was also taking care of myself, ensuring I was alert, ready and prepared for when He spoke; being in His presence as I was opened my eyes to the reality of life. In our day to day lives, we have so many things pulling us every which way and these things infringe on our time with God. Since we cannot see Him with the natural eye, it is easy to push Him aside for another hour or so, until that hour turns to days, weeks and sometimes, months.

Here, I could relax in Him with no distractions. Here, He was always on my mind. The lesson to take from this was when I returned home, to keep Him in my thoughts throughout my day, by continuously speaking to Him and involving Him in the choices I made and the things I would do. On the trip I found this to be an effective way of conversing with Him and this made it hard to forget He existed. It allowed me to get used to the fact that He is real and He is always with me. God should be the first person we share anything with, whether it be joyous or sad. It does not have to be a dramatic gesture but something as simple as an adoring glance up to the heavens as you go about your duties, a smile as you whisper "Father I love you" or a few lines of praise, thanking Him for different things at work, home or whilst relaxing. For each of us, the communication will be different but the common denominator will be communication with Father.

With breakfast, exercise and shower out of the way, I resumed my studies. The topic for the day was — 'The Silence of God'; something we can all relate to and something we embrace with faith, doubt, frustration or fear.

A good question to ask yourself is: why is God silent? And should He be allowed to be silent? I have learned that God can be silent for different reasons but there are two main reasons. First, He may be taking steps to bring us into a deeper walk with Him, causing our faith to be tested and strengthened in the growing process. Second, we may think He is silent but the truth is we cannot hear Him because of sin in our lives, which often stems from us wanting to do things our own way. Only we can be honest enough to admit which is which but we cannot fool God.

If God's silence is due to sin, the easiest way to resolve it would be to confess our sin and make the relevant adjustments in our lives that He requires. God bears no grudges! If His silence is for a deeper revelation of who He is and what He plans to do in our life, then we need to stand strong, keep our eyes on Him and continue to be obedient until He makes His next move.

Blaming God for His silence when we are at fault is a common mistake we make, or maybe I should speak for myself — a common mistake I have made. First, I blame God for not speaking. Then I blame myself for not being good enough for Him to speak to me and before I know it, the voice I am listening to is not God's voice but that of the enemy.

So how do you respond to God's silence? Be honest. Being honest with ourselves is the only way we can move forward; it is also the only way we can truly come before God and expect Him to show up and aid us in our walk to do better.

This was a time to be honest and open, no more hiding. As I began to answer the following question with an open and honest heart, God began to shed light on some of my heartfelt unfulfilled desires, whilst revealing Himself to me.

## Do you expect and look for God to act when you pray?

On reflection, my expectations depended on what I was praying about. Sometimes I attached myself to things that worked in my favour and presumed it must be of God, but I had no real assurance. This was usually the case with matters of the heart-relationships. On the other hand, if it was something specific and practical, for example finances, work or direction, I was more alert, looking for the answers around me, through the Word of God and circumstances but still not as diligently as my studies recommended. I was more confident in the latter because time after time, I had been overshadowed with God's peace in such situations and He always came through for me in those areas. However, when it came to matters of the heart, I often prayed a few times, periodically reminding God of my single status but then refused to pursue the request under the belief that He did not need reminding. At times, I refused to pray because I found it too painful to pray about something that affected me emotionally, only to feel like I was being ignored. On many occasions during those times, God's silence caused me to think Him unfair and uncaring about that area of my life and as a result, the subject of love and marriage become a topic we no longer discussed. I felt abandoned.

**When God is silent, how do you respond and how does it make you feel?**

If it was a practical issue, I continued seeking and believing, confident that God would answer. This is because He had never failed me in this area. The miracles were endless, so once I had His peace, His silence was of no concern. His peace always guided me, His peace was my assurance that He was with me and all was well. Conversely, if the issue was personal, relating to companionship, God's silence usually led to a depressive mindset. This was because I had been praying about this and other personal issues for many, many years and there had been no answers, glimpses of hope or breakthroughs. Sometimes I felt that God was not listening or could not be trusted with matters that where close to my heart. He always appeared silent when I raised these issues and this led to disappointment, which resulted in me refusing to bring the subject up with Him or anyone else.

**What should you do while you are waiting for God to break His silence?**

Well, what I should do and what I have done are so different from each other that they are like chalk and cheese. I should check my life, be honest and repent of any sin that may be hindering His word reaching me. I should continue working on my love relationship with Him and persist in my daily reading of His Word and pray with expectancy. However, what I have actually done is alienate

God from a specific part of my life because of doubt, fear and — I now realise — disobedience.

**At present, is there any sin in your life that would cause God to be silent?**

I am ashamed to say, yes. Disobedience with regard to specific instructions He has given me, which is why I am here, at this point of my life. On reflection, I think my personal desires were never met because of my sin of disbelief. I have just realised when it comes to deep personal issues regarding my heart and love, I do not trust God! This revelation has come as a shock because I never viewed it that way.

**How will you deal with the prohibiting sin in your life?**

Aside from being stunned that I do not trust God with certain aspects of my life, I must repent of my sin against Him and I find myself eager to do so. How could I not trust God when He had proved Himself to me on so many occasions? A few years ago when I was having one of my 'we are not talking about marriage' moments, He told me I was holding up my own process and prior to that, He asked me why I would not let Him heal my heart. Admittedly, I now realise that both times there was a sense of pride in me. I knew He was right but I never really made any adjustments, neither did I take time to think or pray about what He was saying. When He said I was holding up my own process, I briefly asked how and later blamed Him for not answering me or explaining Himself. Now I realise He did answer me. I have been holding up my own process due to doubt, fear and pride and this revelation has hit me hard!

Sitting on my bed, staring at the words I had just written in my journal, I was broken.

I immediately found myself desperately wanting to repent of my sin against God and adjust my thinking to line up with His way of thinking and what He had revealed. What He was showing me made perfect sense, almost like someone had given me a precious pearl. I was desperate to accept the Word of 'truth' in this area of my life and adjust my actions and lifestyle in relation to that 'truth'. I needed to pray and obey; that is to walk in the 'truth' revealed, so that God could work His purpose through me.

As I finished answering the questions, I began to pray. In an act of humble submission, I laid flat on my bed and with a broken heart, I asked God to forgive me. I was so caught up in myself and my pain of disappointment that I had stopped praying about marriage but I was wrong. I remained silent for a while, as the truth behind the lie was exposed.

Then God spoke…

Leaning over me touching my shoulder He whispered softly into my ear *"I want this for you,"* and I melted at

His words. God wanted the blessing of marriage for me. He continued. *"All this time I have wanted this for you because I love you and I have brought you to this place to let you know this because I love you."*

I was speechless, overwhelmed and in awe but not at the fact that God was going to bless me with one of my heart's desire but the fact that He wanted this for me because He loved me. Once again, it was His love for me that took my central focus and I do not think it could have been any other way because love is who He is. Using it as an unstable defence mechanism, I had often confessed that marriage may not be for me because God had never given any indication that I was not to remain single. This was always dismissed by those I shared my opinion with and for good reason — it was not true. Now, the fact that God was talking to me about marriage, backed by the reality that He wanted this for me, was too much to take in. Yet in His presence, all I could do was dote on His every word.

Oh, how He loves me. Tears, tears and more tears as His love ministered to me. He could have chastised me or spoken to me sternly but He did not. He spoke to me in love about His love and His love is better than any blessing He could ever give.

I was so defensive about the subject of marriage, the mere thought of it caused an angry frustration to rise within. My attitude was one of "if God cannot be bothered, why should I be?" I was hurting but refused to deal with the issue. I was too scared to admit to Him what I wanted because in the past, I felt that my vulnerability had been ignored. The many times I cried out to Him from the depth of my anguish, declaring my lonely plight but all I ever got was silence, until now...

The remarkable thing about being on this trip was that whenever God showed me something, everything within me yearned to follow His lead. Every revelation ignited a new thought pattern that was full of life and by accepting it and embracing it without doubt or debate, it took up residence in my heart and mind, breaking up the fallow ground of my distorted mindset and strongholds. No sooner had He stopped speaking, I began to adjust my thinking, by meditating on His words to me and what He had shared with me the day before about love. God was speaking to me as clear as day and that was a beautiful thing. That night my sleep was sweet and during the night when I awoke, I found myself smiling as His words rang aloud in my thoughts. God wanted this for me because He loved me; what an assurance.

> Blessed assurance, Jesus is mine!
> O what a foretaste of glory divine!
> Heir of salvation, purchase of God,
> Born of His Spirit, washed in His blood.
>
> — FANNY J. CROSBY —

# 10

# Love Letters

I awoke the following day with anticipation of hearing what God wanted to say to me. The thought of being tucked away with Him was so exciting; not only did I not hit the snooze button, I was up before the alarm went off. My prayer time was changing from something I needed to do, to something I was excited about doing.

I was learning to sit back, let go and let God lead. In this, I was experiencing that His way of doing things was so much easier than mine, even though it was more challenging. As well as the study 'Experiencing God', I was also reading 'Song of Solomon', which is not a book I had ever paid much attention to. Come to think of it, I had never read it as part of a devotional study, so perhaps you can understand my perplexed concern when God led me to it.

Surprisingly, the book was teaching me about the kind of love relationship God desires to have with us and as I waited in anticipation to hear from Him that morning, He lead me to chapter seven, which is one of the conversations that take place between the lover and his beloved. The jump in chapters seemed a little strange because I was still studying chapter two but as I read chapter seven, I saw the direction God was moving in and I smiled. He knows best.

God is the lover and I am the beloved. He caresses me with His words and they ignite me with love for Him that words cannot express. He goes beyond my knowledge and draws out my private thoughts, answering me in love. It is for this reason that prayer has become an important and exciting part of my life.

Sitting quietly, I began to think about this new and exciting aspect of prayer that I was encountering and as I did so, found myself asking the question "what precisely is prayer?"

Prayer is a connection, a communicative dialogue between an individual and God. In sincere prayer, we connect with God. Prayer is an appointment with God. By appointment, I mean 'encounter'. God is present and He is in your company, whether you sense Him or not, He is there waiting for that one-on-one intimate interaction.

Prayer is where you get to speak, intercede, cry, laugh and even praise Him. It is your time with the Father to petition, appreciate and just as important, listen. It is not just you who has something to say, God has a voice too.

When you set out to speak with someone, be it over the telephone, via internet or in person, you set out to meet and interact with them. It is the same with prayer. In our everyday relationships when we converse, it is a two way dialogue, so too with prayer. When we converse with God, He speaks to us through His Holy Spirit in prayer.

Prayer had been a part of my life for as long as I could remember, though on reflection I am not sure I could have called it all genuine prayer. Feeling tired, weary and burdened, as I sometimes forced myself to get on my knees as part of my morning ritual, could hardly be construed as anticipating an exciting meeting with the creator of the universe, who happened to be besotted with me and could not wait to see my face. In the state I was in, I turned up like I was doing Him a favour, or with the weight of the world on my shoulders. A weight He had already taken care of. I would then proceed to fumble through some words requesting He do precisely what He had already done — lose my chains and set me free. Then when I was done, possibly feeling and seeing no change, I would set off to face the world, leaving God standing arms and mouth wide open unable to get a word in edgeways.

Ok, so it was not always like that but more often than not I did all the talking, whilst God did all the listening.

How can we say that we want to hear what God is saying, if we do not make a habit of allowing Him to speak. Prayer should be a two way dialogue.

Things to remember concerning prayer:

- It is God's Spirit within us which makes us want to communicate with Him through prayer.
- Prayer must be a two way dialogue; we need to give God a chance to speak.
- We need to learn to be still.
- When God speaks, adjust your life to the truth of what He has spoken.
- Show a sense of expectancy — look and listen for ways He will show up during your day via the bible, everyday occurrences, or through others around you.
- Show you are listening and trust Him through obedience.
- God wants to work through us, so let the words "Thy will be done, on earth as it is in heaven" become our desire and not a recital.
- We will experience God when we relinquish the reins and give Him freedom to move.

Remember God cannot help us if we cannot hear what He is saying. If we cannot hear what He is saying, prayer can become a monotonous bore as opposed to an intimate encounter.

Taking all of this into account, I began to humble myself in His presence, becoming less significant as He took centre stage and set the order for our meeting. As I did so, He began to speak to me through His Word.

Lover — *"Oh how beautiful you are! How pleasing, my love, how full of delights!"* (Song 7:6 NLT)

Beloved — *"I am my lover's, and He claims me as His own."* (Song 7:10 NLT)

What a beautiful dialogue. Every word from God's mouth takes my breath away. He has a way of speaking to your depth and stirring up what lays beneath the surface.

Mediating on the scriptures, my thoughts were directed to His deep love for me, as the night before He had told me He wanted me to have the desires He had placed within me because He loved me and now He was telling me I was beautiful. That He delighted in me and I pleased Him. Everywhere I turned, He was pouring His love into me, drawing me into an intimate love relationship with Him. I could not get Him out of my thoughts and wondered if this was the way it was supposed to be? If this was the way He intended it to be? I felt like I was in love. In love with someone who knew everything about me and had the ability to always bring out the best in me.

All day long as I went about my duties, I struggled to focus on anything other than His words to me and they breathed life into me. Truly, in His presence was a beautiful place to be.

I want you to do something for me. Relax and pause for a while. Close your eyes and imagine God telling you He loves you. Despite how you see yourself, He loves you. Imagine His smile, His touch and His words, that kiss on your forehead, His Fatherly gaze of approval as He nods and whispers *"yes, I love you"*.

As humans, we rarely see our good side. We long for companionship, then someone comes along, tell us they love us and we sometimes think of all the reasons why they should not love us. The question we need to ask ourselves is, do we want to be loved or do we want to dream of being loved?

I thought I wanted to be loved but I was dreaming. When I messed up, I condemned and convinced myself that in God's eyes, I was a failure. However, not even my current disobedience, depressive tendencies or suicidal thoughts could separate me from His love. This is a promise found in His Word that Paul spoke of *"And I am convinced that nothing can ever separate us from God's love. Neither death nor life, neither angels nor demons, neither our fears for today nor our worries about tomorrow— not even the powers of hell can separate us from God's love. No power in the sky above or in the earth below— indeed, nothing in all creation will ever be able to separate us from the love of God that is revealed in Christ Jesus our Lord."* (Rom 8: 38–39 NLT)

I tell God I do not trust Him with my heart and He tells me that He loves me, I am beautiful, I please Him and He delights in me. He was drawing me unto Himself so He could show me where I was going wrong because He loved me and in the process, no condemnation was involved (Rom 8:1 NIV). What a privilege it was to be saturated and overwhelmed by God's love, coming at me from every direction.

Exposed to so much revelation, it was hard to act normal. I could not stop smiling. I felt as though I could have burst, as I basked in the truth of His words which brought life to my body and soul. I found myself constantly watching and looking to see where He was working around me, so that I could join Him and assist Him and I did so because He excited me.

As the day went by, He allowed me to cross paths with one of His daughters who like me, admitted she too did not trust Him with her heart. It was only because I was in tune with the Spirit, that I could see where and how God was leading. He wanted her to know His love for her and used me to express where I was, how I got from there to here and what He was presently doing in my life. As I obediently shared, God began to work in her, inviting her to draw closer to Him.

Working together with God was effortless, once I was where I was supposed to be. However, I could not help but wonder how many other opportunities to assist Him I had missed out on, due to my wandering plight.

God loves us all equally and even though it seems like I am the most important person in the entire world to Him, I know without a doubt that you are too. He has the ability to make us all feel special, doted upon and loved by Him, like nothing and no one else matter. He is our lover and He has claimed us as His own.

*Father,*

*I thank You for searching me and revealing Yourself to me, for teaching me about myself, for shedding light on my doubts and fears in such a loving way.*

*You think I am beautiful, which means I am special too, and that means so much to me. I recall Your words to me a while back when You told me I do not realise how beautiful I am and now You are reminding me again. Father You bring a joy, warmth and meaning to my life that goes beyond anything I could desire. Your love touches parts of me I never knew existed, it devours my inner being. You see me and You love me. How many times have I felt like a disappointment to You? Yet You say I am pleasing to You and full of delights that bring You joy. What a beautiful thing to say.*

*I please my Lover, my Lord and He claims me as His own. Father help me throughout the day as I continue to meditate on Your words and adjust my thinking to Your thinking.*

*With love from your daughter.*

I have a friend
A precious friend
Oh how He loves me
He said His love will never end
Oh how He loves me

— REV JOHNSON OATMAN JR —

# 11

# He Loves Me, He Knows Me

Yesterday was so beautiful and today will be even better. That is what being submerged by God's love does, it changes the way you view everything; a welcoming breath of fresh air from my old mindset. Spending time with God on His terms, takes some getting used to and I am learning to let Him interrupt my day as He pleases — and this is Him interrupting my day.

As I prayed this morning, I took to Him all the things I felt He had exposed me to the day before, and asked Him to show me how and if He needed me to assist Him on any matters concerning those around me. He had opened the hearts of others and they had welcomed me into their homes and lives. Was there anything I could do to expose them to His love, by means of sharing and offering hands of assistance? God's work in our life has a ripple effect on the lives of those around us. How it affects them depends on the way we operate.

In submission, I gave myself to Him, to be used as He desired.

After a time of intercessory prayer, I asked the Holy Spirit to lead me in prayer, regarding a friend who had been on my mind. It is important we understand the selfless act involved in interceding on behalf of others. It is just as important that we allow the Holy Spirit to lead us in praying for others and not rely on our own intellect.

Regarding my friend, the Holy Spirit reminded me of the story of Elisha and the Shunammite woman. God rewarded her kindness to His man-servant by giving her a son and began to show me the connection between my friend and the Shunammite woman and what He wanted me to know and do. The realisation of what He was saying could only be received in faith, the very same faith as the Shunammite woman and as His vessel, I also had to have the faith to deliver the message.

Often, we say we have faith in God and all He can do but when faced with the vision of what He wants to do in our lives versus what we want Him to do, where does your faith lay? Looking back at the examples of faith in the bible by way of instruction and prophesy, such as Sarah, Abraham, Joseph, Moses, Gideon, Job, Jeremiah, David, Deborah, Daniel, Noah or Mary but to name a few. Can you honestly say, today — right now — if God spoke to you on a level, as He did to any of the above-named individuals, you would believe, submit and obey with no reservations?

Think about it.

In delivering God's message to my friend, I found myself at a place where I truly believed God was more than able to do what He was showing me, even though it would have been physically impossible. The question was would my friend receive the Word in the same manner I had? If she didn't, would I be tempted to put God back in the little box we often keep Him in and go with the physical reality of the situation, rather than the spiritual evidence of things not seen? Well at first I was tempted to dismiss it because of all the reasons my mind offered as to how ridiculous the Word from God sounded. It went against EVERY natural instinct and all physical evidence. The only basis for support was faith. Not faith in the promise but a deep rooted faith in God. This is the type that can only be birthed from an intimate love relationship with Him.

Grabbing the bull by the horns, I obeyed God and indulged in a very personal conversation with my friend and was able to see Him move in a situation that will bring glory to His name, whilst expressing His love to her.

Communicating with God on this level through the Holy Spirit, should be an everyday occurrence for children of God. We should be shocked when God does not speak, as opposed to being shocked when He does. Often we stifle the Spirit of God with our emotions and limited head knowledge, instead of giving Him the space to live and breathe through us.

Give the Holy Spirit space to move, space to breathe and room to lead.

I continued to pray under the direction of the Spirit for others God had placed on my heart and thanked Him for using me to help bring about His will. As with myself, in the cases of those I was praying for, God's prime motive was to bring them into a personal, intimate love relationship with Him. To draw them closer to Him so that their desires (His desires within them) would be granted in their lives and they would draw closer to Him through the experience. Everything centres on the love relationship with Him and without it there is no foundation to build upon.

Being away from the distractions of everyday life meant God had my full attention and I was surprised at just how much He had to say and how often He spoke. This meant that I was constantly in a meditative state of prayer, praise or reflection.

I was now aware that prayer was a two way dialogue, so His input was always received with joyous ears. God exposed the facts and I made the adjustments and He had a lot to say! Whilst meditating on the fact that I am pleasing to Him and He delights in me, a subtle voice whispered ***"You focus on all the things you can't do while I focus on all the things you can do. When I look at you I see a multitude of things you can do."***

How does He do that?

Out of nowhere, He comes out with these small, sound statements that shed light on vast areas of your life and immediately you see it, you get it and you know it is true.

He knows me so well. Not only did I focus on the things I could not do, I also dismissed the things I could do. I often saw myself as nothing or not good enough and because I chose (did not realise I was doing that) not to dwell on what I could do, my achievements were never in my thoughts. So I was always trying to achieve and please. I did this in my everyday life and in my spiritual life. For years people commented on my strong negative thoughts and questioned why I constantly put myself down but whilst I was aware of this debilitating trait, I was never quite able to shake off, or locate its root or origin. As God began to reveal the truth behind it, it made perfect sense. Not only did it make sense, it was effortless to accept and as soon as I became aware of precisely what I had been doing, I no longer tolerated its presence.

How could I dismiss my achievements?

When God looks at me, He sees a multitude of things I can do and those things make Him smile and nod with immense approval. I bring Him delight and He is pleased with me. Wow, what a compliment! Now I knew what it felt like to have a parent tell you they were proud of you! When God, my Father looks at me, He sees nothing but progress without limitations. All my life I wondered why I thought that way and in one sentence, God spoke a Word and unlocked years of negative thought patterns, to the point where I could literally feel the chains falling.

I needed time to collect my thoughts.

I could not stop my tears flowing, as I began to see the jewels within that God sees when He looks at me. I could not believe how way below the poverty line of God's value I had been living. Every time I thought about the truth He was exposing me to, I could not help but smile with deep assurance, as I rested in Him.

I saw my proud Father looking down on me with great approval. I saw my Lover wanting to be with me and show His affection through His presence and the things He wanted to bless me with — the things that He wanted me to have, not my own selfish desires. Since He wanted me to have them, I found myself resting in the confidence that He knew best. I was consumed by His love, too much to concern myself with who, how, when and what. My Lover, Lord and Father says that I am beautiful. My Lover, Lord and Father says that I bring Him pleasure. My Lover, Lord and Father says that He delights in me. I am my Lover's and He has claimed me as His own.


I am Thine, O lord, I have heard Thy voice,
And it told Thy love to me;
But I long to rise in the arms of faith
And be closer drawn to Thee.

— FANNY J. CROSBY —

*For God alone my Soul
waits in silence…..*

PSALM 62:1 NRSV

# 12

# Reflections

Silence is golden....

As I began to absorb God, His words and His presence, I found myself being introduced to new aspects of worship and wondered what life would be like if I continually dwelt in the secret place of the most High (Ps 91:1). I also found myself wondering how God managed to reveal my thoughts and their origin and answer questions without me uttering one word. Could it be that here, subdued in the presence of the most High, He had become the potter and I had finally become the clay? For someone as desperate as I was to unload and cry out to God, to have found myself speechless in His presence, was quite amusing. The burdens I carried stemmed from unfulfilled desires and misplaced loyalty to God. I was tired of living, hungry for love and desperate to be saved. Though I now had few words, initially I had a lot to say. In fact, it was the uncertainty of knowing where to begin that had fuelled my depression. I came to God's table with so much and yet I had said very little.

Who would have thought sitting in God's presence in utter silence could bring about such healing? The stillness so serene it propelled you into other realms. So beautiful you understood why Jesus often retreated to solitary places to be with His Father.

Being in a solitary place with God causes you to stop doing and thinking, as you to still yourself and relax, breathing in His aroma. As the presence of the Lord consumes you, silence becomes golden. You quit speaking and let Him take control.

At the end of this chapter I encourage you to read Psalm 62:5–8 and meditate on verse five. Allow yourself to come to a place where you accept and say yes, *let all that I am wait quietly before God, for my hope is in Him*" (Ps 62:5 NLT). Recognise and bypass all the distractions of your surroundings and enter into God's place of peaceful stillness.

In the peaceful stillness, His revelations of truth ignited my inner spirit and I was made whole, I was exposed, I was covered, I was forgiven, I was stilled and I was silenced. He showed me myself through His eyes, He exposed my sin, in a way that protected my dignity and I ran to Him to be cleansed. In the peaceful stillness, I found rest for my overweight soul, I found peace for my fatigued body and an endless stream of tears revealed evidence of my brokenness before Him.

After recognising my sins and the distance that I created between myself and God and the emptiness of a busy life, I surrendered. My despair was so intense, I had no choice but to surrender. The desperation for my lover overrode my fear of rejection. I had to find Him. I had to find the one who brought peace, contentment and meaning to my life; the one whose breath of life took my breath away, leaving me speechless. I had to find and worship the lover of my soul.

"Why did I let Him go? He had brought me into a loving relationship with Himself; intimacy beyond my desires and I had allowed myself to lose focus and become enticed by other things. Had I dwelt on my faults, my life would be over. When I was overwhelmed by them, the thoughts of running into the arms of death seemed pleasing. The enemy of my soul had control of my flesh but somewhere, deep inside me, a small seed cried out for the touch of its lover, the water of life. I laid my doubts and fears aside and thought to myself "Only God can help me. He knew my hurts and my frustrations. He was aware of my weaknesses and weariness. He saw the longing in my heart for time alone with Him."

He invited me to come. He drew me unto Himself and His words fed my mind, body and soul, as He led me besides still waters. He set a place of quiet rest before me. He encouraged me to give all of my concerns to Him. *"Don't worry about anything; instead, pray about everything. Tell God what you need, and thank him for all he has done. Then you will experience God's peace, which exceeds anything we can understand. His peace will guard your hearts and minds as you live in Christ Jesus."* (Phil 4:6–7 NLT)

He was the source of all my peace. *"I am leaving you with a gift— peace of mind and heart. And the peace I give is a gift the world cannot give. So don't be troubled or afraid."* (Jn 14:27 NLT)

If we come to Him with our burdens, He will give us rest. Then Jesus said, *"Come to me, all of you who are weary and carry heavy burdens, and I will give you rest."* (Mt 11:28 NLT)

I could continue talking of my experience of His silent rest but what good would that do you unless you experience it for yourself? Maybe then you will understand why my words were few and my longing so deep.

I encourage you to meditate on Psalm 62:5–8 and allow yourself to go beyond words.

*"Let all that I am wait quietly before God, for my hope is in him. He alone is my rock and my salvation, my fortress where I will not be shaken. My victory and honour come from God alone. He is my refuge, a rock where no enemy can reach me. O my people, trust in him at all times. Pour out your heart to him, for God is our refuge."* (Ps 62: 5–8 NLT)

Draw me nearer, nearer blessed Lord,
To the cross where Thou hast died;
Draw me nearer, nearer, nearer blessed Lord,
To Thy precious, bleeding side.

— FANNY J. CROSBY —

# 13

# I AM The I AM

As I leave behind the New York chill and embrace the warmth of the San Antonio sun, I am privileged to encounter another side to God's nature. I am entering a new phase of life, with a change of scenery, a change of pace and unbeknown to me, a change of roles.

We hear and repeat it, often so flippantly it becomes the norm, "God is my everything." But is He really?

Today He is Papa.

A befitting title because today the love that I sense is that of my Papa. Papa's love is unconditional. Papa's love is deep, nurturing and safe. It is all around me and He is the only person on my mind. When I am not alone with Him, I miss Him and as a result, find myself always in conversation with Him.

Landing in San Antonio, unforeseen circumstances created what some would have called a rather pressing and concerning issue. I had two choices, to fret and worry, or to rest in Papa's peace. I knew my flesh wanted to run down panic alley, welcoming all the emotions that came with it but I was enjoying the peace I had been experiencing and would not allow it to be disrupted.

I recalled His teaching in my studies, about dealing with unpleasant circumstances and as I stood in the shower, I closed my eyes and whispered "Father help me to see Your perspective in this situation and not look at it through my own eyes." With my eyes still shut, the sound of running water created a purified stillness. I listened to what I was saying and realised I was growing, I was changing. I could feel myself being enticed to worry but God's peace was too good to leave. I talked to myself, encouraged myself, reminded myself of what I had learnt and why doubting God at this point would be a foolish move on my part. If I gave in at this small hurdle, I would be right where the enemy wanted me to be and then what? The nature of my trip was evidence that God had gone to a lot of trouble to make this all about Him and me; so I could not throw it back in His face by worrying about my present circumstances.

Taking charge of my thoughts, throughout the day, I sought reasons to praise Him and the words that came from my mouth were positive. Was this really me? I hardly recognised myself. As the day progressed, I could not stop thinking about Him and read Philippians 4:6–7 NLT *"Don't worry about anything; instead, pray about everything. Tell God what you need, and thank him for all he has done. Then you will experience God's peace, which exceeds anything we can understand. His peace will guard your hearts and minds as you live in Christ Jesus."* Was Papa speaking to me? As I read, I made my request known and told Him what I needed but requested His will be done, then for the rest of the day I found things to be grateful for.

Whilst on the trip, during the week I made a point of giving God my undivided attention, cutting back ever so slightly on the weekends to spend a little time with friends. Those around me were being influenced by my diligence to seek Him and at the weekends I took time to share what I had learned with them and rest. It was Saturday and all I want to do was run into His arms with my problem and have Him hold me tight. I could literally feel my heart pining for Him.

Around 4pm, whilst out with a friend, the longing to be in His presence intensified and that was when the words, "I need to go home so I can spend time with Papa" came out of my mouth. And for the rest of the day, He was Papa.

Today He wants me to know Him as Papa and today that is precisely what I need.

I have never experienced an intimate loving relationship with my biological father, though things have since changed slightly. However, at the time I had no idea what it felt like to have a loving father who wanted to take care of his little girl, taking whatever steps necessary to make things right for her. That day my lover had chosen to take on that identity and as He did so the silent cry in my heart cried out..."I'm coming Papa, I'm coming."

Words would have been appreciated but if He did not speak, just knowing I was with Him, meant my time would be well spent. Eight weeks prior, I had yearned to be back here, at a place where when I was not with Him, I missed Him and now I was there. What took me five years to try to fix, Papa did in weeks.

Papa....was calm, sweet, personal and gentle, and I became a little child in His arms, allowing Him to treat me accordingly. I cast away my hard 'got to take care of myself' exterior and laid my head on His chest.

"Papa what are you teaching me?"

I felt like the men in the old Testament who built altars in places where God revealed Himself to them, and called that place after the revelation of what they had experienced. Was that what Papa was teaching me? Was this a spiritual bookmark? Was He using my present circumstances to reveal Himself to me as my Papa?"

Thus far, He had revealed Himself to me as my Lover and my Lord but as Papa, His love was different, yet just as deep. I felt like I was His daughter and He was my Father. I whispered "Papa I need this" and as crazy as it sounds, I heard His smile, yes, I heard His smile. I also heard His silence and I knew that He was with me. His smile and His silence spoke a multitude of words to me and all was well. Never before had I seen God in this light, God my Father, but never Papa. Today, He invited me to know Him in a different way and I embraced it with open arms.

At some point in our lives, we all find ourselves day dreaming, particularly us women. You know the scene where you need help or reassurance, you do not know where to turn and you picture the little girl inside you running to daddy, because no matter how old you are, you are always going to be daddy's little girl. Daddy always makes everything better. There is nothing daddy will not do for his little girl and woe betides the person who hurts her! Well today was like that but on a deeper level. Today, I felt Daddy's love in its purest form and I have never felt so safe and loved. Today I knew with immense inner confidence that God was my Papa, that I was His daughter whom He loved and He was going to fix things, purely and simply because I was His daughter and He loved me.

What depth of love.

If your relationship with your biological father is as I have just described, cherish it and give God thanks. You have something many of us, male and female, only dream of.

*Dear Papa,*

*Thank you for knowing what I needed and how best to deliver it. Now I know you as my Papa, I can imagine what it must feel like to have the love of an earthly father. You keep coming through for me, You are changing my heart. You are granting me the deepest desires of my heart, which is to draw closer to You and know You. I gave my life to You when I was thirteen and in the thirty years I have walked with You I have never experienced as many sides to Your character as You are now allowing me to.*

*Today I know You as my Papa and my Papa has everything under control.*

*Like a child I sat on Your lap and rested my head on Your chest and I heard You say "all is well." Our communication was silent as You held me and rocked me as a parent does a small child. Today that was exactly what I needed and You were there. Thank you for loving me. Thank you for this time with You. Thank you for my circumstances that enabled this encounter. Thank you for my revelation and for allowing me to know You through this experience.*

*With love from your daughter.*

When peace, like a river, attendeth my way,
When sorrows like sea billows roll;
Whatever my lot, Thou has taught me to say,
It is well, it is well, with my soul.

— HORATIO G SPAFFORD —

# 14

# The Power of Love

*"Blessed is the man you discipline O Lord, the man you teach from your law; you grant him relief from days of trouble."* (Ps 94:12–13a NIV)

Your laws are precious; Your ways are righteous, Your word breathes life into my spirit. The above scripture is self-explanatory and I can testify to its truth. He was disciplining me in love and He was teaching me His laws. I found strength in His words and His Spirit brought them back to me in troubled times and as I latched onto them, they cast out all fear.

No one really enjoys being disciplined; some of us can hardly handle being corrected! We get defensive, feel awkward, rejected, unloved, resentful, hard-done-by and more. The truth of the matter is, if someone loves you, cares about you and desires nothing but the best for you, they will find a way of correcting you in a manner that should not involve you feeling any of the above. If correction is done right, it should leave you enlightened with a willingness to change and do better. One should never be left feeling guilty or condemned.

As a child growing up, I cannot recall one occasion where I experienced discipline, without feeling one of the above. Discipline was painful, humiliating and sometimes scary. More often than not, it involved one of my parent's strict wrath; in layman's terms 'discipline' meant 'a good beating'. With such memories, it was no wonder I shunned God's presence when I messed up. If my parent's discipline left me feeling apprehensive and worthless, how much more would God's? However, God never made me feel that way, I did that myself by listening to the suggestive thoughts in my head, thoughts planted by the enemy. Seriously, had I known God's discipline could bring about a passionate desire to change and be made right with Him, I would have been the first in line.

Now all I long to do is sit with Him, so that He can feed me, correct me and point me in the right direction. It is good for my soul, my well-being and my natural health. It is living the way God intended. It is intimate companionship with God our Father, not God 'the man upstairs' who seems so far removed from our sense of reality, we might as well be on another planet.

How could I not know God was so loving and what had I done to deserve this?

There was a time when spending time with God seemed like a chore because I never seemed to receive what I wanted but now I loved meeting with Him, sitting in His presence listening to Him speak. His wisdom was profound. When He spoke, it released me, birthing seeds of glorious growth. I hope you are getting this. I hope you are indulging in this as much as I am. Do you find yourself longing for more of Him? Are you hungry and as desperate for Him as I am?

I looked forward to dropping everything and sitting at His table. I looked forward to running into the arms of peace, love and understanding. I looked forward to going behind closed doors, entering the secret place where earth stopped and life began. I looked forward to my time with Him.

It was time.

In silence, I entered my chamber. I prayed and I listened. I began stilling my spirit, anticipating His arrival but nothing happened. I sat and waited and as I waited, my thoughts began to drift, focusing on the studies I had to do. My mind reminded me time was slipping away, "go do your studies; it is still part of Him." I was tempted to listen but I found no comfort in my thoughts.

I felt frustrated that He was not there ready and waiting, as He had been in days past and like waves of the sea, I felt the weight of disappointment sweep over me but before I digressed in its path, I caught myself. I stopped and whispered "Father, make this about You. I am here, what do You want to talk about? What do You want to show me?" I realised I could not leave until He had answered and purposed in my mind that if I had to wait all day, then I would sit and wait. "Father what are You teaching me today?"

My silence was disrupted by my friend's grandma. Grandma was bedridden and whilst in San Antonio, I had the privilege of her company. I was staying with my friend, her granddaughter but it was grandma's house, so if she needed me, I was there. As I sat helping her eat, I asked God again "Father what are You teaching me today?" but He did not answer. When grandma was fed and comfortable, I went back to my room, wondering why the disturbance had not troubled me. Usually I get agitated when my time with God is interrupted but that day I was at peace.

Sitting in silence, I continue to wait, I stilled my thoughts and I waited.

Perseverance…

It took a while, a long while — but He came.

Sometimes you just have to sit and wait and in your waiting do not ever take the initiative, always allow God to lead. Train yourself to sit at His feet and wait. God does not need us, we need Him, so wait and if it takes all day, wait. He is watching your motive, movements and thoughts. Did you know waiting is being obedient? I learned that today. In your waiting for Him to make the first move, you are submitting yourself to Him, which in itself is an act of worship. He will reveal Himself to you when He is ready and that will not be until you are ready.

When your will is not frustrated because He did not come in the speed and manner of His last visit. When your mind is not frantically wondering where He is, why He has not come yet or about the list of things you need to do. When you lay aside your routine, prayer, scripture reading and then departure. When your spirit is calm and you realise this is about Him, clear your mind and settle yourself to wait as patiently for Him as He does for you. Then, He will come. As David said in Psalm 37 *"Be still before the Lord and wait patiently for him."* (Ps 37:7a NIV)

Today He taught me how to forget about myself, concentrate on Him and worship Him.

Today He interrupted my day to make it His own, and He can do that because it is His day.

*Father*

*Continue to teach me Your ways. Continue to teach me how to wait on You, how to forget about myself, concentrate on You and worship You. How many times have I sung that song, "just forget about yourself, concentrate on Him and worship Him?"*

*I now realise it takes a lot for me to forget about myself and ignore my thoughts, but it is only when I do that that I find You. Thank you for visiting me and bringing this true act of worship to my attention. Thank you for revealing to me personal stuff about myself that I had forgotten. Stuff that caused me to see myself differently to the way You see me. Father You restore all things and make them as new, You are the defender of the weak. You comfort those in need.*

*You rise them up on wings of eagles.*

*With love from your daughter.*

Strength will rise as we wait upon the Lord
As we wait upon the Lord
As we wait upon the Lord

— BRENTON BROWN AND KEN RILEY —

# 15

# The Danger of Forgetting

We do not necessarily set out to be forgetful, it just happens. We make promises and with all intents and purposes, we believe in the promises we make. Somehow along the way, sometimes we begin to drift and before we know it the desire, the driving force behind the promise, no longer exists and the promise becomes a dead weight. Something we feel guilty about it or maybe not.

I do not want to forget, I do not want to make promises to God that I cannot keep. I do not want to feel like a failure. I want to be right with God and when trials and tests come, I want to remember to hold onto His words to me and live by them. I am tired of messing up when all I want to do is the right thing by Him. What would happen to us if God looked on the outward appearance and not in our hearts? Where do you think you would be right now if He did not know you better than you know yourself?

If I desire to be sold out for God what prevents me? I can only blame the enemy of my soul for so much, after all you can lead a horse to water but you cannot make it drink. So who is responsible for me forgetting or falling short?

I am.

Thank God for grace, grace that allows me to fall and get back up again. I used to say that I did not want to be in a position to utilise God's grace. I knew it was grace that allowed me to come before God with a broken and contrite heart, repent and then turn around and do better. However, I wanted to do better from the get go; I did not want to mess up at all. I wanted to please God by being perfect and when I could not reach perfection, I turned on myself with condemnation. I now realise that it is impossible to live on this earth and never fall short, and without grace, I would be lost before I even started.

Grace keeps me grounded and humble. Grace causes me to remember the sacrifice Jesus made for me on the cross and the degree to which God loves me. God sent His Son, His only begotten Son, to die for me. Someone else died in my place. Someone loved me enough to take my punishment so I could be free. Those of you who have siblings and have been in trouble, you know, the sort of trouble where you all get called before your parents and the famous question is posed. "Who did xyz?" At which point did any of you willingly take the rap so your siblings could go free? Yet you still love them, right? I'm pretty sure those of you who are parents would die for your kids but what about the person who gets on your last nerve.

The person that dislikes you, lies about you and cannot bear to look at you. Would you die for them? Yet Romans 5:8 explains while we were yet sinners, Christ died for us.

Grace should cause me never to forget.

*Father*

*Cause me to see more and more of what You see in me. Cause me to grow in my surrender to You.*

Lest I forget Gethsemane,
lest I forget Thine agony;
lest I forget Thy love for me,
lead me to Calvary

— JENNIE E HUSSEY —

Lest I forget thy love for me, please lead me to Calvary.

As I meditated on the words of this hymn, God interrupted my thoughts and I welcomed His interruption.

He began to show me my past and the many times He had guided me that I had overlooked. As I watched the scenes I paused and asked, "Lord, was that You?" Glimpse after glimpse, I saw Him at work in my life when I walked with Him faithfully and when I went astray. Truly He never left me or forsook me. As we approached present day, He reminded me of my calling and His revelations to me of my purpose. He caused me to stop and reflect on the words He spoke to me back in 2005 and lead me to scriptures on par with what He had spoken. Ps 139:16, reconfirmed His explanation, *"You saw me before I was born. Every day of my life was recorded in your book. Every moment was laid out before a single day had passed."* Isa 46:11, confirmed His powerful declaration. *"I have said what I will do and I will do it"* I read Ps 139:16 and quickly closed my eyes, as I saw Him at work and sensed Him saying **"it is time"**.

Throughout the trip, as God spoke, I listened and had to adjust my life, thinking, beliefs and walk to match up with His words of *'truth'* so that I could start seeing myself as He saw me. Let me rephrase that, I did not have to but I chose to because it was the *'truth'* as I had never known before. As I embraced His ways, He cleansed and healed me, as His *'truth'* dispersed throughout my life and being.

I heard Him say **"it is time"** and I knew what He meant. It was time to address the problem that caused me to reject His word over my life and run from what I knew to be the *'truth'*. Now that I was making the necessary adjustments to line myself up with what He was saying about me, I had to accept and adjust my thoughts, walk and beliefs to line up with what He was saying about the call on my life too.

My encounters with Him had changed. Now I *knew* He loved me. Now I *knew* He delighted in me. Now I *knew* I pleased Him and my faith and confidence in these beliefs were growing. Now when He spoke, I embraced His words differently because He was drawing me closer to Himself in a way that caused me to take Him at His word, instead of pausing and debating the fact. *"For I know the plans I have for you,"* declares the LORD, *"plans to prosper you and not to harm you, plans to give you hope and a future"* (Jer 29:11 NIV). I had read and spoken that scripture over my life many times but to be honest, they were just words, words that were supposed to make one feel better and trust God. I viewed it as the feel good scripture that people quoted when they had nothing else to say, the same way they used *"all things work together for good to those who love God"* (Rom 8:28 NKJV). However, now it was real because I believed that God truly did know the plans He had for my life and I know with confidence that He wants and thinks good things for me. In order to receive them and walk in them I have to believe, accept, adjust and obey.

Today He wants me to accept my biggest challenge thus far; He wants me to believe I am who He says I am.

*Papa,*

*You know I love You and more than anything, I want and need to please You because being right with You is everything to me. You are life and my soul yearns to please You. Even when I was estranged from You, all I longed for was to be intimate with You. And You have fulfilled that desire and taken me deeper. You have addressed areas of my life that You knew needed addressing; in ways that are enabling me to accept Your Truth about me as the Truth. I surrender myself to You and ask You to help me in my areas of weakness because I need You and all You bring to my life. I cannot go back to the lies and seduction of the enemy because of the damage it causes. It was killing me, literally.*

*Now Papa, here I stand at the fork in the road, where future and life stretch before me, were I am forced to make a decision — What You say about my future or what my past dictates about my future.*

*Papa as I step out in faith, standing on Your Word and all You are teaching and pouring into me, I am given a lifeline. If I do not choose You, I will die and if I do choose You, it means stepping out of the boat on to water. My entire life will change from what it was to what You want it to be. Everything in my life will change and I know You mean EVERYTHING. I will have nothing to rely on but You. There will be no familiarities. Just as You have chosen to draw me to You in a new and different way, so stepping out unto the water by faith into this new era of my life, will be new and different.*

As I released my prayer to God, a sea of uncontrollable tears flowed. Tears of anguish mixed with relief and longing. I longed to be free from a past that had dictated my future for too long. This was a past that had held me captive in my own body. This was it. This was the lifeline I had dreamt of. The time had come. I knew what I was leaving behind and had no interest in reclaiming it. Yet the fear that I felt was not fear of leaving but the possibility of returning. I could not bear to return, if this love I was experiencing was to be short lived, then it was better I stayed in the pit. But I had outgrown the pit. I had manoeuvred every which way I could and there was nowhere else to go. All my life I dreamed of breaking free. I had been a Christian for many years but had never been truly free. Was it possible for me to walk away and never return?

I had come to know God in so many different ways. I was being spoilt by His love and undivided attention. For the first time in my life, I felt I was free to be honest and open before Him. In my pain, I stood naked before Him and seeing all my imperfections, He loved me all the more. He loved me and adored me and wanted to heal my pain. Broken and weary, I took the step and reached out to take His hand.

The room was silent, my eyes were still closed and my tears flowed endlessly. I would never be able to go back to the person I was. I would never be able to return to the lies and deception. I would never be the same again. With my hand in His I knew it was over, there would be no going back. Regardless of what lay ahead I was now on higher ground. The foundation upon which I stood was a solid foundation built on love and I was safe.

*Papa, I see You smiling at me, no words, just Your smile. And in Your smile, I see Your love. I am never going back Papa, I am never going back. Promise me You will hold me tight, I never ever want to go back. This isn't just about the call on my life, it is about everything. With this step I embrace everything, all my desires that run deep. Desires I did not even know existed and the life and relationship with You, that the enemy told me I could never have because I was not good enough.*

*Papa You are still smiling. I am overcome with emotion of Your love for me and I am broken.*

*Papa I surrender. I have given myself to You before but I have never totally surrendered. I surrender to You and all You have for me, Your way. These are not just words.*

*You search my heart and know all things, so You know that I truly surrender. You did it this way so that I would surrender and that makes me surrender even more (if that is possible). I surrender and I rest in Your arms. Somehow You make stepping out of the boat and on to the water safer than staying in the boat. By adjusting my life to Your Word and stepping out of the boat, I embrace all that You have for me according to YOUR will.*

*I love you Papa.*

It's a new season It's a new day
A fresh anointing is flowing my way
It's a season of power and (spiritual) prosperity
It's a new season coming to me

— ISRAEL HOUGHTON & DERRICK W. THOMAS —

# 16

# The Power of Doing Nothing

After the events of the past few days, I find myself in a place I have never been before. I find myself doing nothing.

I am not stressing, I have no concerns, I am not even thinking. My mind is clear — completely clear — and I am at peace. This is the kind of peace that illuminates your entire being and radiates from the inside out.

Imagine having nothing on your mind but peace and contentment. If this is what being totally consumed by Christ is like, then heaven is beyond words. My soul is full of God's Words: Words of discipline that ignite love, Words of peace that bring reassurance, Words of wisdom that activate growth, and Words of truth that breathe life.

Today as I do nothing, I realise how much of my time is taken up with the things that cause me to be distracted and somewhat disconnected from God. These are the things that obscure my vision from my surroundings, the very surroundings God inhabits. In the busyness of the day, we miss Him in the warmth of the sun, the moisture of the rain, the quietness of untouched snow and the coolness of the wind. We miss Him in the vibrancy of the thunder, the stillness of the night, the magnificence of the moonlight and the calm sound of running water. We miss Him in the blessing of seeing a new day and all that He desires to teach us and expose us to throughout that day. We ask Him to teach and help us but we do not stop to take heed, listen and learn. So how can He teach us?

Our minds cry out for peace and quiet and we think nothing of it but we need peace and quiet, we need to make time to do nothing. Absolutely nothing.

In God's presence, I was learning of the difficulties involved in stilling myself, whilst growing aware of the many distractions life threw in my path to keep me from doing nothing.

When I do nothing, God has my full attention.

Please understand I am not telling you to give up and sit around all day doing nothing, that would be encouraging you to be lazy. No, I am encouraging you that when away from the secret place throughout your day, stop and make time to do nothing, even if it is for only five minutes. Be still, empty your mind and do nothing but breathe. With practice, you will be able to discipline yourself to let go (do nothing) and let God be.

Much strength is gleaned in the secret of doing nothing, the secret of being still and silent. You begin to see how much of your time with God is 'you-orientated' and how much is 'God-orientated'. You begin to recognise the enemy's distractive traits, catch yourself and dismiss them. You become aware of the importance of listening to God, as opposed to just talking at Him and the more you yearn to hear from Him, the more you learn to be still and do nothing.

As I did nothing, He filled my day with so much of Himself, I was overflowing. I wanted to stay there with Him but I knew at some point I would have to go back to everyday living and I realised things would have to change, in order for me to create the correct balance for my life. The reality is that whilst keeping busy can keep you out of trouble, it can also keep you out of God's presence. Make time for God and allow Him the freedom to set the schedule. Remember — He is the creator and you are His creation.

Today He allowed me to digest things thus far, to meditate and soak up His revelations. Today as I did nothing, He reassured me of my cleanliness and right-standing with Him, and encouraged me to learn from Him. Today He showed me my old habits could be broken and I could be delivered from the bondage of my past and that new habits and attitudes could be established if I listen, trust and obey.

*"Whatever you have learned or received or heard from me, put into practice. And the God of peace will be with you."* (Phil 4:9 NIV)

Trust and obey
For there's no other way
To be happy in Jesus
But to trust and Obey

— JOHN H. SAMMIS —

# 17

# The Perfect Gift

Father, before You give me anything, give me You. These are not just words, they are my heart and God who knows my heart knows they are true.

You may be wondering how I can say "Father, before You give me Your promises or any of my heart's desires, give me You." It is easy to say this when you have encountered the Lord intimately because you come to understand that God's gifts are not as important as God Himself. Having His gifts does not mean He is present in your life and not having Him present in my life, for me is misery. Nothing fulfils me, nothing has true meaning and nothing is significant, without God. I am thankful to God for allowing me to encounter intimacy with Him because if I had not, when I strayed away, I would have drifted into nothingness. In those dark times, it was the remnants of our intimate encounters within me, which cried out for Him and not the desire for things He could give me. Yet prior to those encounters with Him, it was the desire for things He could give me or things I felt would make me happier, that I longed for.

The truth is, once you truly encounter God, nothing fills you like He does. That said, why then did I stray, given the events of my first trip? I strayed because I tried to help God do what only He could do and when things did not work out as I imagined they would and should have, I second guessed God. Then when He was silent, I blamed Him and held Him responsible for not bringing to pass what He had shown me. I tried to use my own abilities and attributes but they failed. I constantly confessed that I did not have what it took to be used or called by God, which was true but it was never about what I could do but what He was going to do through me. My doubts, disobedience and lack of confidence in my own abilities led me further away from Him, whilst memories of our encounters together reminded me of what I was missing. I tried to ignite the encounters but when my attempts failed, I became depressed and concluded that I was a disappointment to Him, that He had revoked my purpose and I was lost. Yet still I yearned for that intimacy.

It was the war between my yearning for Him and the way I saw myself before Him that kept me bound and when I went before Him, I was wrapped up in so much guilt and self-condemnation, anything He said rebounded straight off me. Then I blamed Him for not helping me.

Thank God for His faithfulness and His unfailing love. I thank Him for bringing me to this point and place and for doing it His way.

Whilst away, as I came to the close of my study 'Experiencing God', I was humbled, touched and honoured to be having my deepest desire met. God was not only allowing me to encounter Him, He was engulfing me in love, exposing my errors and teaching me at the same time. He was revealing Himself to me in the order He saw fit and not according to my agenda. Marriage was the last thing on my list but it was second on His. Ministry was the second thing on my list but He had it further down on His — and His way made sense. It healed, enlightened, challenged, and revealed, all at the same time.

Prior to the trip, I was in a very dark, heavy place. Every day I felt like my life was being sucked from me. Everything was an effort. Sometimes I would lie in bed without washing for days, only leaving my room to get food. Some days I would not even eat. I did not talk to anyone. I just lay in darkness thinking about my life, what I had been through, what I wanted and why it had not happened. Questions about what was the point of trying and what people thought of me, consumed me. I was becoming invisible, barely existing. Galatians 5:1 calls it 'being burdened with the yolk of slavery' and I could not have summed it up better. It was a dark place, where death seemed like the only answer and for me, it was torture. Amidst my doubts and fears on one hand, fear of God would not allow me to take my own life, whilst on the other, guilt, self-condemnation and disappointment argued it was the only way. Even after it had been agreed with work that I could get the time off for the trip, I was still burdened. After attending a wonderful watch night service on December 31st 2010, the following day as I rested in bed, I visualised myself jumping off the ninth floor balcony at work.

It was a new year, I had been offered a new start and I had my upcoming trip to look forward to. I knew once I got away I would be ok, that somehow I would find God but what if I could not find Him? What if nothing changed? That evening, the words in my head were stronger than ever. They told me all I had to do was find enough courage to climb out onto the ledge and they — it — would do the rest. Knowing once I stepped off there would be no going back, I watched myself falling, like a hovering bird in slow motion, to the ground.

How could suicide look so peaceful?

The more I thought about it, the more I felt myself being wooed into a trance to take my life and I was not afraid. I think it was the reality of what I could have allowed myself to do that snatched me away from my suicidal thoughts, crushing the heaviness and dispersing the darkness and the shame that led me to believe I was a disappointment to God. I was in trouble and at that point I knew that if I did not take drastic steps to rekindle my love relationship with God, my family would be attending my funeral.

I had to lay aside all my guilt, condemnation and all the negative thoughts that hovered over me whilst I tried to resume my love relationship with God. I had to forget about the many failed attempts and focus on what the love relationship and intimacy meant to me. I purposed in my mind that what I once had, I could have again and I knew regardless of the cost, I had to get it back. I had to create new habits, godly habits. During the twenty one day fast, I spent time repenting and humbling myself, whilst focusing on my desire to reignite the intimate love relationship I once shared with the Lord. Anyone can say they have a relationship with God but can you honestly say you have an intimate love relationship with Him?

So here I was, on my spiritual getaway and I had a lot to be thankful for. I knew what I had, what I allowed myself to lose and what God had given back to me and what He had given me is better than what I had before.

That is why I say "Father before You give me anything that is part of Your plan or purpose for my life, please, please, give me You."

Searching for a lifetime for something to satisfy
Paid a lot of prices and so many nights I cried
In my time of desperation
Came the simple revelation
That was all I ever really wanted
Was You In a time of second chances
What I found at second glance is
That all I ever really wanted was You

— DONNIE MCCLURKIN —

# 18

# Too Many Words

At the hottest part of the day, the Texan sunshine was almost unbearable and many ran for cover into air-conditioned buildings. However, I wanted to bask in it and make the most of the heat I rarely got to experience back home. As I walked around the local neighbourhood, I noticed the intricate details that made one house different to another and the huge sports utility vehicles that adorned almost every drive. I noticed the playing fields designed specifically for children and the patriotic residents who hung the flag outside their home, proud to be American. I noticed the various trees, the fruit they bore and the pretty cherry blossoms in bloom.

The sun had not reached its hottest peak for the day, but already in the 90's, the streets were empty, which is a pity because there was so much beauty out here to see. The sky was a striking blue, not a cloud in sight and the only sounds I heard were the natural sounds of nature. The birds sang a sweet melody and the bees hovered from flower to flower, while the tiny lizards ran for cover at the sound of my footsteps.

What a way to say good morning!

I love to walk and take in the sights but today in my walking, I realise I notice a lot more when I am silent. If I were to take the same walk whilst on my mobile phone or walking and chatting with a friend, would I notice all the things I noticed this morning? I think the answer to that is 'probably not'.

So what was so special about silence?

As I walked, I did not feel the need for words, in fact on the few occasions I attempted to muster up a conversation with God, it felt as though He was urging me to hush. At first it felt a little weird. How can you go on a prayer walk and not talk? However, as I walked I began to notice things, detailed things. Each attraction caused me to notice something else, which in turn ushered my focus entirely towards God and before I knew it, He was ministering to my unspoken requests. Until today, I never realised how beautiful grass is or how striking a cloudless sky appears. I never noticed the little things in nature that play a major role in everyday life. Until today, I never realised that when I am in God's presence, I often talk too much.

Please understand I am not saying that we should always come before God in silence or use few words when we pray. No, just like in life, there is a time and season for everything, as Ecclesiastes teaches us. So in our prayer lives, there is a time to intercede with passion and authority, a time to lament, a time to talk to God passively and a time to be silent.

Back at the house, sitting in my room, gazing out of the window, I felt the sun's heat growing stronger and stronger and its warmth on my face felt good. As I closed my eyes, the different shades of reds and orange I saw were so beautifully enchanting, I could have sat there forever. Without realising, I was stilled and undisruptive, precisely where God wanted me.

Then He spoke.

*"I love to look at your countenance, it says so much without you uttering a single word. I look on the heart not on the outward appearance."* (1 Sam 16:7 NIV)

As I listened in silence and stillness, I felt warm tears rolling down my cheeks. One sentence from Him and I am broken.

Understanding that God often wants to just look at me; His child whom He loves, is quite something. He does not always require a barrel of words, sometimes He just wants to gaze at me, spend time with me and show me things that are a reflection of who He is. He wants to delight in my presence as much as I want to delight in His. He wants to bring to the surface my deepest desires that lay hidden within. God wants to love me His way, not mine. He wants to take me by the hand and lead me. He wants, He wants, He wants; it ought to be all about what He wants.

So what precisely does God want?

As the day progressed my words ceased to flow. My agenda held no weight in His presence. He was feeding me, feeding me from the inside out. In silence, my prayers were being answered but how was I praying without speaking?

Silent prayer is something that needs to practised and is a powerful source of prayer; it is God in total control. It is where God's Spirit meets with our spirit and our wills become one. It is a place where head knowledge is not a requirement but total submission takes centre stage. It is the place where we cease to be and enter into His courts. It is the place where we become less and less and He becomes greater and greater.

If like me, you have a heart for devotion and love to spend time alone with God, then I urge you to ask Him to lead you into silent prayer, the place where visions are exposed and flowing tears bring joy, healing and restoration. If like me, you love to hear the sound of God's voice more than your own, then I urge you to step out in faith and allow the Holy Spirit to lead you into the realms of silent prayer. It is the place where you can listen and learn as He teaches. It is the place where you hang on His every word.

Often we try so hard to help God do what only God can do. As we cannot physically see Him, we feel the need to do something all the time. If He says be still, we try to think of all the things we can do to be still, aside from just being still, then we wonder why it is not working. Being still includes not thinking!

I recall the numerous times I have told my nephews and nieces not to move and then watched them watching me, to see if they can move an inch without me noticing. Each minute movement they make is greeted with my words, "I said do not move!" well I guess that is us humans all over. God says do not move but we think 'He means do not get up and walk away', so we sit there rubbing our face, swaying from side to side, humming to ourselves and do not realise, being still means 'being still'. Do not move, means do not move! Be still and do not move!

In preparing ourselves for time with the Lord, to go deeper into silent prayer, the only thing we have to do is the only thing we can do, still ourselves and cast down every disruptive thought that enters our mind; that is what preparing ourselves is all about. God will do the rest. We do not have to set the scene and disrupt our thoughts, by trying to figure out how He is going to come or if He is going to come; just submit, be still and practice being obedient. God instructs us in this when He says, *"be still, and know that I am God."* (Ps 46:10 NIV)

As I sat trying to still myself and not doing a good job of it, I felt a frustration rising within and if I had not caught the seed of frustration and cast it down, I would have been led astray. After a while, I realised I had to silence my entire body as well as my mind. I had to cease existing.

Then He spoke.

*"Sometimes when I am silent it is because I am looking at you, smiling with approval. Silent prayer is not just about you being silent so I can speak; it is also about sitting in my presence, just you and Me in silence."*

When couples are in love, on many occasions they sit in quietness, snuggled up close to each other, savouring the enjoyment of each other's presence. We need to learn to love God the way He wants us to love Him, with a love of silent quietness, a love of humble submission and a love of total surrender.

*"Let all that I am wait quietly before God, for my hope is in Him. He alone is my rock and my salvation, my fortress where I will not be shaken. My victory and my honour come from God alone. He is my refuge, a rock where no enemy can reach me."* (Ps 62:5–7 NlT)

Can you honestly say that you allow all that you are to wait quietly before God?

For me this was not always the case, in fact until now, it had never been the case. I had heard of silent prayer and read about it, I even practised it but I never submitted to it. Today I realise its powerful roots stem from the fact that it is the only time when spirit meets spirit and our wills are intertwined.

In silence, God was teaching me the discipline of being silent and continued by telling me I needed to practice being silent, so that He was free to lead. In a firm, yet loving voice He said *"you have done enough,"* and led me to meditate on Proverbs 3:5 NLT *Trust in the Lord with all your heart, do not depend on your own understanding.* As I meditated, He led me back to words He had previously spoken to me and directed me to meditate on them also.

*"You focus on the things you cannot do while I focus on the things you can do."*

*"Trust in the Lord with all your heart; do not depend on your own understanding."* (Prov 3:5 NCV)

*"When I look at you I see a multitude of things you can do and those things make Me smile and nod My head with great approval. You bring Me delight and I am pleased with you."*

*"Trust in the Lord with all your heart; do not depend on your own understanding."* (Prov 3:5 NCV)

I was so caught up in myself and my pain of disappointment that I stopped praying about marriage. Then He softly whispered *"I want this for you."*

*"Trust in the Lord with all your heart; do not depend on your own understanding."* (Prov 3:5 NCV)

*"For I know the plans I have for you, says the Lord. They are plans for good and not for disaster, to give you a future and a hope."* (Jer 29:11 nlT)

*"Trust in the Lord with all your heart; do not depend on your own understanding."* (Prov 3:5 NCV)

By meditating on His words and scriptures, I was feeding myself with *'truth'*. This was the *'truth'* that in time would destroy the stronghold of lies that for many years controlled my life and as we sat in each other's company He continued to speak ***"You are too hard on yourself."***

I could not hide; He knew everything, every detail about me. He knew my strengths and my weaknesses and exposed them in ways that made me want to run to Him, hug Him and hold onto Him for dear life. When He speaks, He opens you up to revelations as He sees it and speaks *'truth'* into your life. I am so glad He is my Father and that He knows me so well.

I cannot recall the amount of times I have been told by others "you are too hard on yourself" but I always justified it with an answer. I thought God expected better of me and set the bar so high that not even I could reach it. Why do we act like we are the God of our lives and when will we start looking at ourselves through God's eyes?

Humbled, grateful and tearful, I asked God to help me in this area of my life and help me adjust my thinking to His way of thinking. I did not want to be responsible for blocking His love from reaching me, especially when His love was the only thing that kept me going.

*"Trust in the Lord with all your heart; do not depend on your own understanding."* (Prov 3:5 NCV) do you think you can do that? Can you trust in God with all your heart, with every fibre of your being? Can you do it with no reservations, no discussions, doubts or fears? Do you think you can will yourself to do nothing but trust without relying on human understanding? Do you think you can allow yourself to push aside any distractive accusations that come to mind and purpose yourself to trust in the Lord with all your heart and not depend on your own understanding?

Oh, the pure delight of a single hour
That before Thy throne I spend,
When I kneel in prayer, and with Thee, my God
I commune as friend with friend!

— FANNY J. CROSBY —

# 19

# Lest I Forget

The flesh wants what the flesh wants. It is gluttonous and rebellious and strives to hold on to things that often serve it no purpose. The Spirit on the other hand, is gentle, calm, peaceful, vibrant, powerful, kind, faithful and extremely patient. Unless we implement our free will, the spirit of itself will never try to overrule the flesh. The flesh on the other hand, will attack everything in its path just to get what it wants. It is only as we take charge of our free will, that we are able to overcome our fleshly desires.

The understanding of this concept got me thinking, "why did God give us a free will and how do you use yours?

I decide whether my flesh or the Spirit gets the use of my free will and as much as I would love to tell you it is always the Spirit, I cannot. There are times when I allow my flesh the freedom it desires out of greed, fear, doubt or sheer disobedience, to name a few. Yet the Spirit remains calm and patient. I wish my flesh would do the same! The flesh is selfish, always wanting to be the focus of attention. It is always thinking it knows best, and if you do not ground yourself in the Lord on a daily basis, rest assured your flesh will fool you. It will not give up without a fight. The question is, are you prepared to fight back?

In my time alone with God, I was still learning to be still and wait. After years of doing things my way, my flesh was reluctant to give up its post as chief instigator. Rather than be still, it actively planted triggers that caused me to believe I should have been doing something when I was supposed to be being still. I heard my thoughts loud and clear and admit they argued a strong case. I needed to read the Word. I needed to spend hours in the Word, learning about God. I needed to pray and talk and keep talking, I needed to be active. My flesh told me enough to hold me in condemnation, when at first I did not oblige and neglected to remind me that God had told me to practice being still and silent before Him. I tried to recreate the experience from the day before but yesterday was gone and I was powerless to create God's presence or set the scene. My mind told me being still was being lazy and forgetting what God told me, I gave in to the arguments of my flesh. I tried to get into the Word, only to feel even more unsettled and frustrated. It did not make sense. I cried out "Father I need You. I need Your Word. Open my spiritual understanding, so I can hear and see what You are saying to me." Nothing happened. I continued reading but the frustration intensified. I may as well have been reading a foreign language!

In tearful anger and desperation, I told myself I was not going back; I was not going to give in to the emotions of failure. I opened my 'Song of Solomon' study and tried to pick up from where God had told me stop but the same unsettled feeling greeted me. I read for a while and researched the scriptures but nothing gave. "Father," I whispered "I cannot take this, yesterday I felt so close to You and today I can't even get into Your word, what is going on?"

He remained silent.

I took out my journal and read my insert from the day before and as I started to read, my peace returned. Silence. I had forgotten to remain silent until He said it was time to do otherwise. How could I forget?

Closing my eyes, I began to still my body, mind and soul and as I did so, I sensed His peace and whispered "teach me Papa, teach me."

How easily we forget. I was so busy trying to please Him that I forgot to be obedient. "Can you believe that?" It took discipline to be still and I was beginning to realise it also involved surrendering. Papa was teaching me the joys and discipline of surrendering everything to Him, the correct use of my free will and what happens when I allow Him total control. Finally, I was at rest. Finally, I had His peace. Finally, I was in His will.

Silence and surrender.

*Dear Papa*

*You know all things. Thank you for showing me my mistakes. Thank you for placing a desire in me to find You. As I learn to wait and be silent before You, help me to remember everything is always about You. My time with You is about You, not me. Father this is a new discipline You are instilling in me and though it seems hard right now, I know it is possible because You have initiated it. I am happy now because I have Your peace all around me and that is what I live for. Thank you for answering my prayer and for being faithful. I love You and look forward to learning more about You and making the necessary adjustments required to hold onto Your peace.*

*When I think about the way You are dealing with me, it causes me to cry. There are so many sides to Your character. There is so much depth to Your love. My mind, body and soul needs to feast off You. The more time I spend with You, the more I see who I am supposed to be.*

*Continue to teach me how to make it all about You, I look forward to sitting at Your table in future and having You look upon me in silence as You observe me in Your love and teach me how to love You with a submissive heart.*

*With love from your daughter.*

It is alright
As long as I have my Lord beside me
It is alright
As long as I have His hand to hold
As long as He watches over my soul
As long as I'm under His control
It is alright

— CARIBBEAN CHORUS (AUTHOR UNKNOWN) —

# 20

# Everyday People

As my time in San Antonio drew to a close, I could not help but dwell on all the things God had exposed me to. There are no secrets with God. I can hide parts of my life from those around me. I can deny inner pain and joy. I can even fool you into believing I am something that I am not but I cannot hide from God and for that I am thankful. I am thankful that I have someone with whom I can be real. Someone with whom I can just 'be' and by that I mean someone I can sit in silence with and they just know. Without me speaking a word, they just know. Believe it or not, not talking actually takes the pressure off of trying to explain. In humble silence, I can take the most difficult situation to God and without uttering one word He sees, knows and helps me. There is a depth about the silence that speaks louder than words.

My late mother used to say there is a time and a place for everything. Solomon teaches us the same thing in the book of Ecclesiastes. In prayer and communication with God, there is a time for words, a time for tears, a time for praise and a time for silence. As you develop your intimate love relationship with God, He will lead you into various ways of communication and you will begin to know and sense the time and place for each medium.

I have come to realise that it is during my silent time with God that He speaks to the deepest parts of my life. The areas that I do not allow anyone to see, the areas I try to hide from myself.

*'Order my steps in Thy Word, and let not any iniquity have dominion over me.'* (Ps 119:133 KJV)

> *Father take Your rightful place in my heart, as I trust You and let my roots grow deep down into Your love and hold me strong. You have set before me everything I need — Your wisdom, discernment, love, faithfulness, intimacy, unchangeable promises and more. I love the way You invite me to sit with You so You can feed me and give me Your rest.*

I wanted to be obedient, I wanted to learn how to wait and be silent. This could have taken all day and if it did, would I have felt useless? Maybe, but who cared! I began by meditating on a confession list I had drawn up, confessing God's spoken word over my life. At times it seemed a little tedious but I knew I it had to be done. I continued praying and praising God through my confessions, taking time to digest and reflect and as I did so, I sensed myself ceasing to exist.

I spent some time praying for friends who were sick, asking the Holy Spirit to guide me and interceded on their behalf.

Still in His presence, we broke for lunch, which was interesting because it was like having a lunch date with God. I had never thought about having lunch with God before and have to confess, it really is something special. After prayer, He suggested lunch and accompanied me to the kitchen. Ok, so you may be thinking this part a bit far-fetched but it was as real as real could be and I was loving every moment of it. The more time I spent with God, the more sensitive to His leadership I was becoming. The more real He was becoming, the more wonderful our time together was.

During lunch, I found myself thinking about His words to me two days before, when He told me I was too hard on myself and as I pondered, He read my thoughts and began to speak. *"When you mess up, you condemn yourself so much and in doing so, you block My love reaching out to you."* His revelation was short, precise and to the point. His truth was so powerful. It made sense but I never realised I was hurting myself, I thought I was helping. I thought being hard on myself kept me in check. When I messed up, I could not get past the standards I set for myself, the standards I believed God required of me.

*"You judge yourself harsher than I judge you and when you do that, you do not allow me to love you."*

"What? I judged myself harsher than God judged me? If I judge myself harsher than He judged me that meant...." He finished my sentence. ***"That means you do not love yourself as much as I love you."***

Another revelation hit home!

*Father thank you for Your help, You are faithful.*

*With love from your daughter.*

Shackled by a heavy burden neath a load of guilt and shame
Then the hand of Jesus touched me
And now I am no longer the same
He touched me, oh He touched me
And oh the joy that floods my soul
Something happened and now I know
He touched me and made me whole

— WILLIAM J. GAITHER —

*For God alone my Soul
waits in silence.....*

PSALM 62:1 NRSV

# 21

# Vulnerable Honesty

With the Texan sun behind me, I embraced the heavenly sunshine of Orlando, Florida — my home away from home. How I loved this place. The heat, beautiful scenery, palm trees and bright skies all made the way for a slower pace of life. What more could a girl want?

It was b-e-a-u-t-i-f-u-l!

Then Jesus said *"Let us go off by ourselves to a quiet place and rest a while."* (Mk 6:31 NLT)

Thus far, my time away had been enriching but as I sat on the balcony of my villa, it was almost like we (God and I) were on our spiritual honeymoon.

Throughout the trip, I had been with God behind closed doors and even though I was listening, obeying Him and reaping its benefits, I had not completely shutdown, stopped and come to a complete standstill. Up until this point, I thought that what I had been experiencing was awesome but this, right here, right now… words failed me.

The sun was shining and I saw God in everything. My entire surroundings were a reflection of His greatness. It was so peaceful, the harmony of natural sounds, with just the two of us there to make use of it's offerings. He was enjoying my company and I was learning the treasures of being silent and still before Him. He is so quiet, yet vibrant and powerful. There is a stillness about His silence that causes your entire being to hush and one glimpse from Him reveals a million things you would have never known about yourself.

My deepest desires were being fulfilled. This was what I had longed for. His words were true. He could do more than I could think or ask. I could have never found the vocabulary to put into words and request what He was allowing me to partake in, to be still and know that He was God. The longing in my heart was for more of Him, all of Him, as much as my body could take in of Him. Not just while we were there together but always, every day. Life without God was not the life for me.

I had made God into who I thought He was. I had belittled His greatness. I had sinned against the Lord God Almighty and yet He still loved me. As I looked around, all I could see was His love.

*Father,*

*I want You to know me, as a man knows his wife when he is intimate with her. I want You to ignite the parts of me that are dead to me — spiritual stimulation. I want You to consume every minute of my time away with You.*

*I had been going against Your will for me because I did not trust You with my will. I refused to think, dwell or believe in what I wanted because I did not trust You with my heart and all the time You wanted the same things for me. I wasted so much time believing a lie. I gave the enemy permission to torture me and sought other means trying to attain my desires, when all I had to do was trust You. I refused to speak to You about marriage because it hurt so much. I fought against You and when You tried to stir up the desire within, I pushed it away because it was too painful. I told myself You were not listening but it was me who was not listening. I refused to listen to others when You used them to speak to me and I refused to listen to You when you spoke to me direct. I drew my own conclusion of what You were thinking, based on my own distorted perceptions. I was rejecting Your will for me. I was fighting against You for no reason. Rejecting Your will almost cost me my life, all because I believed in a lie.*

It is a dangerous thing to know God and reject His will.

As a child, I daydreamed and longed to be married and after my mum died, I longed for it even more. It had been over twenty two years since I first spoke to God about marriage and during that time I managed to talk myself out of it because I would not trust Him with my heart. When He told me He wanted this for me, I was crushed and delighted in His love for me more than marriage itself. As I sat there in His presence, He opened my eyes to the depth of my disobedience and explained that marriage was not just for marriage sake; it played an important part in His will for my life.

Once again, I was silenced.

For the longest time I needed a breakthrough, like it was well overdue and I guess it was. It was as if my life, the way God planned (my utmost desires), stood before me. All I had to do was reach out and take it but in all my reaching, my hands never stretched forward enough and I never understood why. Today I understand why. I was not just refusing to think about marriage, I was rejecting part of God's purpose and plan for my life. Since He spoke to me, my thoughts and belief on marriage have changed. I now believe this is something He wants for me because He loves me and because He has told me so but I never ever thought it played an important part in His plans for my life. As I sat listening to all He was revealing. He explained that I would make a good wife and mother and that it would bring out more of Him in me, His best in me. What could I say to that? If it were you, what would you say?

I cried.

I had been in battle with the enemy of my soul for over twenty two years on this matter and I was tired. When I came on this trip I had not expected this. I thought I would pray about my doubts and fears, ask God to help me believe in Him for a husband and He would oblige. Who would have thought I was the problem and that all the time God was waiting on me. Now I understand what He meant when He said I was holding up my own process.

I am learning that regardless of what we think or feel, God is the Beginning and He is the End. He knows all things and He can do all things.

When I left London, I knew what I needed. I had no words or descriptions but I knew I needed to live and breathe and find a reason for doing so. I had come to the end. I knew I loved God, I knew He was real but I did not love and trust Him with all my heart, mind, soul and strength. Now I was learning from the Master Himself. I was being taught as He restored my soul.

*Papa my prayer today is.....*

*Let all that I am be silent before You, so that I can be still and know that You are God.*

Everyday He reveals a little more of Himself to me and I hope He is doing the same for you.

I hope and pray God is ministering to you in areas of your life and that your relationship with Him is being challenged. There was a time on my trip when I questioned who was I that God should go to such lengths for me? I am now beginning to understand, all of this is but a mere fraction of what living for Him should be like. That means I can look forward to everyday life like this. I know there will be days when He may seem distant. There will be days when I am challenged by what I believe. There will be days when my time with Him will not be as lengthy as my time with Him here. However, if I have to take just one thing from this entire experience, it would be that God loves me, He knows me and He will never forsake me.

For me, God had always been real but now He had stepped into my life and made it personal. He had shown me how and why He loved me and given me many reasons to trust Him more than ever. That said, I could still lose it. Just because I was having a wonderful time with Him, did not mean from there on in everything would be smooth sailing. I am not being negative, I am just keeping it real. I know I will be tested. At some point in my future, everything God has said, done and revealed will be challenged by the enemy.

Now, I could write in bold letters, "hey devil, bring it on!" I could invite him to test me right here, right now. Chances are I may win the battle but this is not about boasting in my abilities to get one over on the devil. In 1John 4:4, the bible explains that we have overcome because of who lives inside us, not because we ourselves are able to do so.

There is strength in the dependency we have in God that causes us to become childlike and that is what God is looking for. So when the time comes for me to be tested, I will hold onto God's love for me. I will remind myself of all of this and my time away with Him. I will rely on the prayers of others covering me but most of all, I will recall that God will never leave me or forsake me. Regardless of how it looks or feels, He is always with me and His word will not return to Him void but will accomplish what He sent it forth to do. (Is 55:11)

Make sure you are always on the same page as God, and not chapters ahead or behind.

Guide me O Thou great Jehovah
Pilgrim through this barren land.
I am weak but Thou art mighty
Hold me with Thy powerful hand.
Bread of heaven, bread of heaven
Feed me till I want no more
Feed me till I want no more

— WILLIAM WILLIAMS —

# 22

# You Think You Know

*"The Lord is my Shepherd; I have all that I need. He lets me rest in green meadows; He leads me beside peaceful streams."* (Ps 23:1–2 NLT)

If I had to describe my time in Orlando, that scripture would have summed it up perfectly. It was so peaceful; it felt like God was saying *"just rest"*. His presence was strong, occupying every inch of space and His silence added a stillness that dominated my attention. Everywhere I went, He was there. Sitting by the pool, I saw Him in the beauty of His creation. As I sat on my balcony, His presence captivated my breath, so much so that if we spoke, it would have disturbed the atmosphere. This constant and strong sense of His presence was new to me but it was all part of who He was.

Although I was getting used to just sitting in His presence, there was still a part of me that wanted to make sure I was following His lead and not just being lazy, enjoying the scenery. So I found myself constantly surrendering, asking Him to take the lead and reminding myself that this was His trip. There are so many sides to God; it would be impossible to skim the surface in this lifetime and from time to time, I caught myself silently repeating the words, "what did I do to deserve this?" The more I asked the question, the more He showed me His love.

Whilst at church a few days ago, a pastor spoke on a message entitled 'follow the Spirit's lead and believe God to do what He said He will do.' This was a fitting word and right on par with what God had been teaching me. 'Follow the Spirit's lead.'

I awoke the following day with thoughts of his message running through my mind. What did it mean to follow the Spirit's lead and how could I accomplish it? Preparing myself to be taught, I began by reading John 14, 15, 16 and Galatians 5 and started to see the Holy Spirit in a new light. After meditating on the scriptures, I realised that I had spent most of my life ignoring the Holy Spirit. It sounds crazy but it is true. I knew He was there but I scarcely relied on Him as I should have. When I prayed, I went direct to the Father my way and when the Spirit tried to assist me in prayer, I sometimes ignored His direction. I did not always allow the Spirit to comfort me and when He reminded me what God was saying or tried to teach me, I did not always listen. I did not treat Him as a person, I saw Him as a thing but as God began showing me the role of the Holy Spirit, I started to realise how precious He was to my daily walk. He is a spiritual being that God has given to us to support, counsel and lead us. The Holy Spirit plays a vital part in our lives, yet we often run to God and leave Him behind.

Gal 5:25 says *"Since we live by the Spirit, let us keep in step with the Spirit."* We are to keep in step with Him and follow His lead. In Jn 16:7 Jesus explains it is for our good that He goes away and if He did not go the Holy Spirit would not be able to come to us. Whilst Jn 16:13 ESV tells us *"When the Spirit of truth comes, he will guide you into all the truth, for he will not speak on his own authority, but whatever he hears he will speak, and he will declare to you the things that are to come."* When Jesus ascended into heaven, God the father sent the Holy Spirit as our aid to lead us in all things. So why, oh why do we treat Him as though He is invisible, non-existent even?

As I sat, He was with me. While I ate, He was with me and if I stopped acting like I knew it all, He would guide me. Surrendering to the Spirit does not make us weak and helpless, it merely makes our flesh weak and helpless. In this way we choose to walk by the Spirit and not by the flesh. It is only then we can become less and less so He becomes greater and greater. It is only then we can grow in love, peace, patience, joy, goodness, kindness, gentleness, faithfulness and self-control.

As the day progressed, I pondered on how I could adjust and change my attitude towards the Holy Spirit and God started to reveal some things to me about the way we think, of which I for one am guilty. He said we want to know everything! If He is going to do something, we want to know how it is going to be done. We want to understand what He is doing and how long it will take. We want to know too much!

"So what is wrong with that?"

According to God, a lot! If He shows me everything He is doing and I know everything about Him, He ceases to be God and I no longer need Him. That was quite a lot to take in for someone who thought they were kind of ok with the way God worked. Yes, I admit there were times when I posed the 'when, how and why' question but was I really that bad? Did I do it that often? After spending such quality time with God, you would think I would be ready and used to His questions but when He asked me, *"why can't you just trust Me to know everything and take care of everything?"*, I was speechless. He went on to explain *"that is what makes me who I am."*

I thought about it for a long while and then realised how stupid I had been. God was right (of course). If I was to know all the things I wanted to know about Him, in particular when it came to waiting and receiving by faith, what would be the point of His existence? As hard as it seemed, all I had to do was trust God for being God.

God equals the unknown, beyond what I could think or imagine. He has no beginning or end. He cannot be contained, held hostage, bribed or fooled. He made all things and without Him nothing was made that was made, so how on earth do we expect to understand that and more? Why can we not concentrate on accepting God by faith? My confidence should be in Him being all things and knowing all things. My assurance should be in Him being able to do the humanly impossible. He knew me before I was born, while my earliest memories of life start from the age of three.

It's ironic; parents tell their kids what they need to know, on a need to know basis and nothing more. If they want to do something and the answer is no, they do not always give a reason. However, the reason is that more often than not, they know best. Often it is because they were once that age, so they know the pitfalls. Other times, it because the child just would not understand. Have you ever had a conversation with a child that continues to question you? "But why? But why? But why?" Well it is a bit like that with God and us, only on a higher level. Unlike our parent's knowledge, which is limited, God knows EVERYTHING! And does not have to tell us EVERYTHING! But we want to know EVERYTHING.

We make it difficult for ourselves, due to our lack of faith in God. We try to understand Him in our flesh instead of allowing the Holy Spirit to lead us, thus enabling our inner man to comprehend the things He wants to make known to us. All we have to do is believe in Him as God and rely on the Holy Spirit's help and have faith in His abilities as God and not our own human understanding. Just accept that He can do ANYTHING because that is what God does. No arguments. Adjust, accept and believe!

Sounds so simple but in the flesh, it is impossible, which is why we are supposed to keep in step with the Spirit and follow His lead.

I have a friend who works in IT and anytime I have a problem with my computer, I go to him for help. I do not expect him to tell me he cannot help me because as far as I am concerned, if it is not working, it can be fixed and he can fix it. The words "it cannot be fixed" do not exist! Using this analogy, God showed me that I had more faith in my friend's capabilities to do the impossible, than I did in Him — and He was right. The good thing was that now I knew I was capable of trusting without doubting, all I had to do was direct that trust to the right person — God.

If I know everything there is to know about everything God does and is, He ceases to be God. It is knowing all those things and more that make Him God and should make me want to trust and rely on Him. There is no point in me sitting here trying to figure out how He can be omnipresent and omniscient. Firstly, I would never be able to understand because He made me, not the other way round. Secondly, if I knew how He could be omnipresent and omniscient, then I could use that knowledge and be omnipresent and omniscient myself, not to mention other ways I would find to use it to my advantage. What need would I then have for God if I knew everything?

Keep in step with the Spirit and follow His lead! Time to go and reflect.

*Father*

*I make it harder than it needs to be. It all sounds so simple and it is. In Matthew 11:30, You said Your yoke is easy and Your burdens light and when You explain things the way You have, I see how easy and light it is. I now realise that without the Spirit, I am helpless.*

*Father, forgive me for omitting Your Spirit's help from my life and at times trying to go it alone. I have caused myself needless pain and thrown Your help back in Your face. Have mercy upon me.*

*What did I do to deserve what You are doing for me? Your love truly is unfailing.*

*Holy Spirit assist me at all times, everyday in all that I do, so that what I do I do unto the Father and not unto man. As I submit to You and keep in step with You, I look forward to growing in love, peace, joy, patience, goodness, kindness, faithfulness, gentleness and self-control. I look forward to learning how to trust God as God and stop trying to understand Him with my flesh, trying to be my own god. May Proverbs 3:5 be imprinted in my mind, may I daily trust in the Lord with all my heart and not depend on my own understanding.*

*Father, thank you for making me lie down among green pastures as You restore my soul. Truly You are God, for if I had tried to imagine all of what You are doing for me right now, I would have come up short. Father, I know You want me to relinquish everything and place all my trust and confidence in You and I know with the help of Your Spirit, it is possible. With man it is impossible but with You, all things are possible.*

*Father, I cherish all that You are saying to me, keeping it close to my heart so that I will not sin against You. Thank you for explaining to me the precious role of the Holy Spirit. Thank you for granting me my heart's desire to know You. You are causing me to overflow with humble gratitude. Your peace sweeps over my soul and I am still and silent before You. I am humbled before You. You are my Lord, You are my God. You are my Lover, You are the I AM and I rest in Your arms.*

*Allow me to embrace more of You, allow me to know You.*

*With love from your daughter.*

Here I am waiting, abide in me, I pray
Here I am longing for You
Hide me in Your love, bring me to my knees
May I know Jesus more and more
Come live in me all my life, take over
Come breathe in me,
I will rise on eagle's wings
Come live in me all my life, take over
Come breathe in me,
I will rise on eagle's wings

— REUBEN MORGAN—

# 23

# Shhh...Let Him Teach You

Good morning Papa....

I am confident that the sole purpose of my trip was so God could clean me up so He can dwell within and what a clean up it has been. Each day I encountered something new.

In the bible when God speaks of His ways not being our ways, neither His thoughts our thoughts, I think we often take it for granted. Something happens that we cannot explain or understand and to comfort ourselves or others, we quote that scripture. Yet on other days, we act like we know all God's ways and thoughts. The reality is we only know what He wants us to know and when He wants us to know it. Just because He came through in a particular way for that job you needed last time, does not mean He will come through the same way next time around. Yes, He has traits that we recognise and our spirit bears witness to but let us not put God in a box and act like we know all there is to know about Him. Remember it is the unknown that makes Him God.

As His children we are told that we, His sheep, listen to His voice. That means we recognise His voice. *"My sheep recognise my voice; I know them, and they follow me"* (Jn 10:27 MSG). Notice the scripture says we recognise His voice but He knows us. Having an intimate relationship with God enables us to recognise His voice and get to know Him intimately on different levels, it does not mean we know precisely how He thinks and acts.

In Genesis 22, God told Abraham to sacrifice his only son, Isaac. As we read on we understand this was a test but at the time Abraham did not know that, yet he was ready and willing to obey. So what made Abraham obey such an illogical request? Based on His promise to Abraham, does that sound like something God should have requested of him? God had promised Abraham a son and told him countless generations would be birthed from him through that son. Be honest, if God had made that same promise to you, then told you to kill your son (the only heir to the promise) how would you respond?

I doubt Abraham understood why God made such a request but what he did know and recognise was the voice of God. He recognised that the same voice that told him he would have a son, was the same voice that told him to sacrifice his son. Abraham knew he could TRUST God, he had FAITH in God and BELIEVED in God's promise to him. It wasn't until the angel stopped him from killing Isaac, was he aware that God was testing him.

How well do you know the voice of God?

There are countless examples in the bible of things God did and said that did not make sense to those He spoke to but His purpose was always fulfilled through their actions, once they obeyed. It is my belief that Abraham and others like him in the bible, had an intimate personal relationship with God and the relationships were put to the test. I know there are many others that the bible speaks of but for me, there is a lot I can learn from Abraham.

So what am I saying? I am saying that when we make our intimate personal relationship with God the most important thing in our lives, when we make time to stop and learn to listen in prayer as opposed to doing all the talking, then we will get to *know* and *recognise* the voice of God. When that happens, no matter what God asks of us, we will be more than happy to oblige because we know the one who makes the request of us.

In my short life, God has made some requests of me that seemed ludicrously insane and I obeyed because I recognised His voice. On the other hand, there have been times when He has requested a simple act, something that made perfect sense and I deliberated, doubted and sometimes disobeyed. Whether logical or illogical, the latter always happened during times when my relationship with Him was anything but intimate.

Spending time with God is a wonderful thing and hearing His voice, well that is priceless!

*"Forget the former things; do not dwell on the past. See, I am doing a new thing! Now it springs up; do you not perceive it?"* (Isa 43:18–19 NIV)

I think for most, the hardest thing to do is change and by that I mean do something different to get the same result or an even better one. Often if a system works for us, we like to stick to it and rarely explore other avenues. So, my question to you is, when it comes to God would you say sticking to what YOU know, works best?

God was trying to teach me something new, something that did not quite make sense to my thoughts but the fulfilment it brought my spirit was overwhelming. Sitting in the Florida sunshine, all He required of me was that I sat in silence. This was a simple request but how would you feel if you had to sit in silence before God for the whole day?

Silence…

What started off as one day turned into numerous days and as the week progressed, the atmosphere was one of complete stillness and silence. Stillness and silence overshadowed by deep nurturing unconditional love. Our words were few but yet we were one. "Surely God could not expect me to remain silent doing nothing for an entire week?" but why not, who made the rules, me or Him?

His thoughts are not my thoughts and His ways are not my ways.

God wanted me to spend an entire week sitting with Him in silence, whilst resting in His peace. My spirit was eager to oblige but my thoughts struggled to come to terms with His request and periodically searched for logical things for me to do with my time. A day in silence, I could understand but an entire week! I tried to find things to do. I read the word and spent time in prayer. I tried to fill my day with things centred on Him. It was ok but I was far from settled. In pursuit of peace, I searched myself. Jemma, be silent! Be still. Be submissive. Relax and do nothing. Remember not your will but His. He has brought you to a beautiful place where you can be silent and rest, so be silent and rest. Give up and give in.

I was still learning.

Then Jesus said *"Let us go off by ourselves to a quiet place and rest a while."* (Mk 6:31 NLT)

As God taught me new things. I found myself being fulfilled in ways one could only describe as incredible and realised the silence was necessary because there were no words in my vocabulary suitable to express what was happening. It was as though my limited use of words would have offended and disturbed the atmosphere. I urge you to still your entire being before Him in worship and allow yourself to move beyond words, into a place of solitude and silence. This is a place where you can embrace the secrets of intimacy. I urge you to let go and find the effortless trait of merely abiding in Him. Shh, let Him teach you.

Imagine being alone with God in the most beautiful setting He can find, just the two of you. Imagine your mind totally cleansed from everyday distractions, only Him occupying your thoughts. You think something, He smiles looks at you and finishes the thought for you. You are one! I am trying to articulate the mood of where I was but I am struggling for words, so I am going to let you go and experience it for yourself. Go spend some time with Papa, He is waiting for you.

Be still for the power of the Lord
Is moving in this place
He comes to cleanse and heal.
To minister his grace.
No work too hard for him.
In faith receive from him
Be still for the power of the Lord
Is moving in this place

— DAVID J. EVANS —

# 24

# Testing, Testing 123...

*"He escorts me to the banquet hall; it's obvious how much He loves me."* (Song 2:4 NLT)

When God invited me to His banqueting table, I had no idea there would be such a vast variety of food, the most exquisite of venues, first class service and bespoke itinerary. Everything was absolutely beautiful. The amount of knowledge He exposed to me was more than I anticipated. More than I dreamed of. More than I deserved.

You may have been blessed by my writing thus far but when all is said and done, I have to live this. God did not give this to me just so I could share it with you. He gave it to me because He desires the best for me. He wanted me to make the relevant changes in my life so I could come to the place where He could commune with me. I have been given much but not more than I can handle. When I think about what He is doing with me, I draw comfort from His love for me. His Words have set me free from a lifetime of bondage.

The changes He makes in us are for our good!

I am free. I no longer have to place needless pressure on myself, trying to reach humanly impossible standards. I do not have to focus on trying to accomplish all the things I cannot do, instead I look forward to the multitude of things that God says I can do. I do not have to be scared to talk about marriage; my heart has been set free from the thorn bushes that entangled it. It is ok to think that I am beautiful, it is even better knowing God thinks I am beautiful and He delights in me.

This was such good wholesome food!

I knew where I was coming from, the way my mind worked and reacted. I knew how precious this time was to me and I did not want to miss one moment of it. Of late all Papa had requested of me was silence in His presence and it was not for me to wonder why but more to anticipate new dimensions of our relationship. I was used to being the instigator but if I wanted to go deeper in Him, I had to release the reigns.

Today was challenging because today I did not sense Him anywhere and it is hard to want more of God and feel like you are not quite hitting the mark but after all that had happened, I had to hold on to what I had been taught and meditate on it.

Now was my crisis of belief; time to put into action what I had learned. If I am honest, at that precise moment I was not sure if I was supposed to be still or do something and although I felt a sense of "what now?" trying to weigh me down, I chose to hold onto what I had learned and filled myself with His 'truth'. I chose to wait on Him. It was challenging being in a place where I could not feel Him, when for the past month I had constantly been saturated with His love. However, it is like that some days and He said that He would never leave me or forsake me, which means He is with me, even now.

*Papa, help me to remain still and quiet in you, to explore a new side to your character, to be still and know that You are God.*

*With love from your daughter.*

Yea, though I walk in death's dark vale,
Yet will I fear no ill: for thou art with me, and thy rod
And staff me comfort still.

— SCOTTISH PSAITER —

## 25

# Your Choice

*"As the apple tree among the trees of the wood, so is my beloved among the sons. I sat down under his shadow with great delight, and his fruit was sweet to my taste."* (Song 2:3 KJV)

Have you ever sat under God's shadow, reading the word in faith, love and prayer, quietly meditating on Him and His instructive words?

It is a beautiful thing for two main reasons. First, during that time, God has your undivided attention and is able to teach, fill and enrich you at His own pace. Second, you can relax in His presence with no distractions.

Today I invite you to make plans to set aside a large portion of your day to hang out with God. If you have children, make arrangements for a babysitter. If you have plans, cancel them. Make a sacrifice, take a day's holiday from work, go somewhere and spend some time in God's presence, allowing Him to set the schedule. Trust me, you will not be disappointed!

Today I leave you to sit in Father's presence, to read His word and absorb His *'truths'* as He ministers to you. I know He has a lot He wants to share with you, so go be with Him. Sit at His feet and worship Him in total surrender. Give up your will for His, your thoughts for His, your life for His.

It is your choice.

Enjoy!

Here I am Here I stand Lord,
My life is in your hands Lord,
I'm longing to see
Your desires revealed in me
I give myself away
I give myself away
So you can use me

— WILLIAM MCDOWELL —

## 26

# Calvary

It is my belief that the greatest book you will ever read is the bible. Though it is not a book you can comprehend solely, depending on your natural understanding and at times, it is not an easy read. Today it took me most of the day to read Jn, 3–11 and I had to read it relying on the Holy Spirit's teaching and guidance. As I read, I realised many times when I read the bible, I am looking for what I want to get from it and not what God wants me to get from it. Often, we read saying we need a word from the Lord but what we really mean is we want God to tell us what we want to hear — an answer to a specific issue.

As a young Christian, I often opened my bible randomly, believing the scripture my eyes fell upon would be a direct word from God. This was ok when it fell on some form of promise. However, when I was in real need of comfort from the Word and ended up reading the genealogy of Christ with names I could not pronounce or something in the Levitical law that bore no relevance to my situation, I was left devastated.

Reading the bible should not be entered upon as a quick-fix solution to a problem one is experiencing. It should be approached with the same reverence and respect as when approaching God in prayer.

Today as I read God's Word, I approached it with a desire to know and understand what I was reading. As I read I saw how much Jesus relied on His Father in His ministry, so much so, my flesh wanted to cry out "ok, I get the message" but did I really get the message?

In the Gospels, many of the people were so caught up in what they felt they knew about God and the law, they dismissed anything Jesus had to say. Standing on the outskirts and reading about it, it was easy to point the finger and see their mistakes but are we not guilty of the same thing? The bible says they did not hear and believe because they did not know God, (John 8:47) and when I do not listen to God and doubt Him, it is because I do not know Him either.

Knowing, listening to and obeying God's Word got me thinking about whom I entertain on a daily basis. As a chef, I love to cook and sit and enjoy good food with good company and I pictured myself sitting down to eat and inviting the enemy to sit and eat with me. Sounds insane but that is precisely what I am doing when I choose to listen to the enemy over God. My question to you is who is sitting at your table? Who do you generally hang out with and entertain? Whose report do you believe? Furthermore, who do you generally imitate?

I recently watched Mel Gibson's 'The Passion of The Christ' for the second time and still cringed at certain scenes. As I watched, with one eye open at the horrific scenes of unjust, inhumane treatment inflicted upon Jesus, all I kept thinking was You (Christ) went through all of that for me.

One of the things that hit me hard that I missed before, was the reality of God's love for us. The bible says that He is love and love was evident in its purest form, when Jesus is shown having nails hammered into hands and in between the anguish and excruciating pain, He whispers, almost as if His life depends on it: "Father, forgive them for they know not what they do." In His pain, all He could see was our small mindedness and how we think we know but we do not really know. Jesus knew that if His accusers really knew who He was and what He signified, they would have been hailing Him as King but here they were putting Him to death because they did not know.

In a calm, childlike voice, He pleaded with the Father to forgive His killers. He was innocent, dying to save man from their sins and man was the one who killed Him. He cried out: "Father forgive them, they really do not know or understand what they are doing. It is not their fault; they are blind, so please forgive them." It was this, His passionate plea to His Father that resounded in my thoughts as I thought about His death on the cross.

*"There is no greater way to love than to give your life for your friends."* (Jn 15:13 THE VOICE)

At times our minds can become overcast with the needless jeering of the enemy, always in our ear enticing us to feed off our emotions. Someone upsets us, he plants a host of not so nice things we would like to do or say to them. Someone hurts someone we love and he feeds us a million and one ways we can get back at them. God asks us to do something, the enemy encourages us to question God. God tells us something, the enemy tells us to forget about it, suggesting we cannot trust God, mainly because we cannot see Him. Yet we cannot see the enemy either!

I have often pictured Jesus having one of those moments as He approached His death. From the time Judas betrayed Him, to the point He breathed His last breath, I cannot imagine Satan leaving Him alone for one second. Imagine having to hold down the fact that you are the Son of God! You are the Son of God and you have a host of heavenly angels back home, ready and waiting to obey your every command but you have to put up with your own creation insisting you explain yourself! You can call thousands of angels to defeat those who have you in chains but you cannot because you are the Son of God and you love your Father too much to disobey Him. You are the Son of God and would be well in your rights to declare "do you know who I am?" moments before You choose to release fire and brimstone upon a rebellious people but You cannot because Your Father is relying on You to save the very people who are about to kill You. You are the Son of God, You control the universe, You created the people who sit in judgement over You and You do not say a word. You are the Son of

God but You cannot get angry, lose Your cool and tell Satan where to 'go' because if You do, You would be right where he wants You. You are the Son of God but You remain calm and humble, like nothing fazes You. Yet hours before You were crying out to Your Father; asking Him if there were any way possible He could remove the cup from which You were about to drink from You. You are the Son of God, yet not Your will but Your Father's will be done.

There was no cursing, no shouting and no outbursts of anger. If I am honest, Christ's behaviour in the lead up to His death, puts me to shame. Right down to the last minute, all of who He was, was always on display. Love in its purest form.

A few chapters back I asked how many of you would be willing to die for someone who disliked you and without jumping to conclusions, I doubt there was a large show of hands; that said I think we all need to go back to the cross and learn from our Saviour. It is not just that Jesus died for me that gets my attention, it is the way in which He conducted Himself as He was being crucified that causes me to close my eyes and lower my head in an element of shame — shame that desires to do better.

Whilst I thank God for Mel Gibson's portrayal of Christ's crucifixion, I am reminded that the bible says God can do more than we can think or ask. Whatever we can think, He can surpass way beyond our knowledge. Once again this got me thinking. In that case, the scenes I had just watched, many of which I had to turn away from, were probably a lot worse than the film could have ever depicted and it is that which breaks me and reduces me to tears.

We cannot begin to imagine the scene, starting from the beating He took. Remember those that sought to kill Him, hated the fact that He claimed to be the Christ and His humility whilst on trial no doubt infuriated them even further. Even Peter who swore he would die with and for Jesus was petrified and denied knowing Him. Yet Jesus made sure when He rose from the dead He specifically sent word to Peter, reassuring him He still loved Him and wanted to use Him. What love.

They spat at Him, gave Him a beating that should have killed Him; I am sure many had died from a lesser beating. Then they forced Him to carry a heavy cross on His raw beaten flesh, mocking, jeering and still beating Him along the way. To be honest, at this point in the film, I wanted to jump in and hurt someone and found myself shouting "leave Him alone", yet through all that pain, at no time did Jesus say or portray anything negative. He never complained and He did not ditch the cross for an easier option.

We rejoice and are thankful that He died for our sins and rose again but to me what Christ went through for us, to be thankful is not enough. If you really want to thank Him, surrender your life back to Him and by surrender I do not just mean accepting Him as your personal Saviour. I mean *really* surrender your life to Him, daily, total surrendering your will to His will. Not my will but Yours, Lord. Imitating Him and giving Him free reign of your thoughts, actions and words. That is total surrender, can you do that? I, for one, am going to try my hardest.

*Father*

*When I try to imagine what Christ went through for me; I cannot find an image that fits. The Son of God was crucified and I cannot imagine that the enemy made it an easy task.*

*But Christ remained faithful to the end, He bore the pain and disgrace and He never once complained, yet I complain over the slightest thing.*

*Father You have given me a new life in Christ and I give You my life to have full reign. I lay down my selfish desires and give everything to You. I will not use fancy words and long prayers but just as Your mercies are new each day, so each day I surrender my will to Your will and submit to following the Holy Spirit's lead.*

*Papa I cannot make Jesus' death be in vain, for in doing so, I too become one of his killers. Jesus I show my overwhelming gratitude by giving my life back to You so that Papa can use it for His glory.*

*Amen.*

*With much love and my life, from your daughter.*

In Christ alone,
Who took on flesh fullness of God in helpless Babe
This gift of love and righteousness
Scorned by the ones He came to save
Till on that cross as Jesus died
The wrath of God
Was satisfied for every sin on Him was laid
Here in the death of Christ I live

— STUART TOWNEND —

# 27

# Affirmation

As I enter the last week of this glorious getaway, I am more than thankful for the way God has been moving in my life. It is easy to *say* that you have changed but it is more encouraging to see the changes in you as they appear. When I think about the horrendous place I was in, not just over the past six years but also the effects of the strongholds that had me bound, my tears reveal the depth of my joy. Alongside this, my daily commitment and surrender to my Father displays my overwhelming gratitude. Now 2nd Cor 5:17 takes on an entirely new meaning. For me it has become reality. I am a new creation, all things have been made new. *"Therefore, if anyone is united with the Anointed One, that person is a new creation. The old life is gone — and see — a new life has begun!"* (2nd Cor 5:17 THE VOICE)

I am a new creation, I belong to Christ, my old life is gone and my new life has begun! My deepest desires have come to pass and I continue to work on the changes daily, while digging my roots down deep into Father God and applying His Words to my life. In this way, when the storm bellows it's gusty winds, I will be like the house that was built on the rock!

*"Therefore everyone who hears these words of mine and puts them into practice is like a wise man who built his house on the rock. The rain came down, the streams rose and the winds blew and beat against that house; yet it did not fall because it had its foundation on the rock. But everyone who hears these words of mine and does not put them into practice is like a foolish man who built his house on sand. The rain came down, the streams rose, and the winds blew and beat against that house, and it fell with a great crash."* (Mt 7:24–27 NIV)

Papa has really taken care of me and I pray He has done the same for you too; I have been and continue to be, spoiled by His love.

I have been set free by Christ and I am free to live. I am free to rejoice. I am free to worship. I am free to love. I am free to trust and be happy in Christ because Christ has set me free and the Holy Spirit, my comforter and counsellor, leads and guides me into all of God's truths about me.

Anyone can sit and write a compilation of feel good words to encourage one's soul. Anyone can research and teach the scriptures in ways that open up one's understanding as never before. Anyone can call themselves a child of God. Anyone can call themselves a Christian. Anyone can talk the talk... but it takes a really sincere person to say what they mean and mean what they say.

If at the end of this I go back to my old life, more fool me. God could not have done more than He has to get my attention. If at the end of this, I turn around and say, "but did God really say that?" Shame on me! What then would it take to convince me that God is alive, He can be trusted and He loves me? If at the end of this, I do not fight to hold onto the precious gifts God has given me, then I am nothing but ungrateful. If from here on in I believe it is all going to be plain sailing, then I have learned nothing.

*"For I am persuaded, that neither death, nor life, nor angels, nor principalities, nor powers, nor things present, nor things to come. Nor height, nor depth, nor any other creation, shall be able to separate us from the love of God, which is in Christ Jesus our Lord."* (Rom 8:38, 39 KJV)

This is not an act, neither is it a fictional narrative. This is my life. It is as real as real can be and I have to live it! To whom much is given, much is required.

I know there will be good days and there will be challenging days but I love the Lord and I desire more than anything to please Him. Over the past seven weeks, He has poured so much into me to edify myself and others. So as I pray for all of you who will read this and be challenged by it, for those of you who will be transformed by it and for those of you who may find it a little too overwhelming, I ask that you open your hearts. Open your hearts to what you have read and allow God to minister to you and take time to share and encourage others in the faith. This road we are on can be hard at times but we ought to look out for one another and show each other the same love that Christ shows us. *"A new command I give you; Love one another. As I have loved you, so you must love one another."* (Jn 13:34 NIV)

*"Carry each other's burdens, and in this way you will fulfil the law of Christ."* (Gal 6:2 NIV)

This is God's Word to us so let us not take it lightly.

Where would I be if not for Your grace
Carrying me through every season
Where would I be if not for Your grace
You came to my rescue
And I want to thank you for Your grace
Grace that restores
Grace that redeems
Grace that releases me to worship
Grace that repairs visions and dreams
Grace that releases miracles
Your grace

— ISRAEL HOUGHTON & AARON LINDSEY —

# 28

# Home Time

I have been doing a lot of 'talking' and I pray that you have learned a lot and are encountering new dimensions in your relationship with God. It would be hard for me to believe you have not been challenged or moved by any of this because every time I go over my own writings, I am forced to stop and reflect as God continues to minister to me. His Words are full of life and I believe this book is full of His audible Word.

I am so thankful that God loves me and can honestly say He has saved my life!

My trip has taken me to different parts of America. I first travelled to New York, then San Antonio, followed by Orlando and now Virginia. Each place has brought different sceneries, experiences and revelations. Each home has offered me nothing but love, kindness and peaceful rest. I have encountered different climates, different accents and different laws. Each day has brought new mercies from above and opportunities to soar to higher heights with our Father.

I am my Father's child and I want Him to be proud of me. I am my Father's child and I want Him to recognise me. I am my Father's child and I want to place my hand in His and keep it there.

The thing I love the most that has been abundantly available to me throughout my time away, is my conversations with God. I love to hear the voice of God, it keeps me alive. When He speaks, everything is unlocked and the word 'life' takes on a whole new meaning. If you want to know what fulfils me and makes me happy, it is hearing the voice of God revealing things that only He can, and awakening areas of my life that make up the 'me' He predestined me to be.

When I described my life as something that was slowly dying, I was not exaggerating; I was literally killing myself with negative strongholds from my past.

Instead of seeing my strengths and the many obstacles I had overcome in life, I saw a continuous array of obstructions and embraced the weariness each one brought. I believed in God but I also believed in the pain of my past. The two could not occupy the same living space, so one of them had to go. It was not that I did not want to let go of my past because I did; only God knows how much I wanted to be free but the burden was so heavy and I often disregarded it, thinking I was insignificant.

I thank God for granting me the desires of my heart and for setting me free. I thank God for the tranquillity that is experienced when I am still in His presence. I thank Him for the overwhelming ambience that ignites when He is present. In my time away, many of the points He has raised were areas of my life that no one but myself and Him saw. These are areas I thought would never be resolved because every time I tried to break free, I ended up right back at the same place.

If only I had trusted Him with my heart!

Brothers and sisters, do not live in the past. Do not believe the lie and do not overlook your worth. You are too special to sit there and die. If I had died in my state, what would have become of this book? If I had committed suicide as was suggested, what spiritual legacy would I have left behind? My testimony is one of endurance and forgiveness and the lie stops here!

Today is the last day of my time away; it is time to go home. Stirred up within is a passion and desire to live out what I have been taught and who I am in Christ. To be set free is quite daunting. To notice the changes within is a blessing. To continue on the path I am on is my assignment and one I intend to work on with all my heart, body and soul.

The bible says in Jn 14:15 that if you love God, you will keep His commandments. If I love God...

Love, is not a word but something that is real, something that is displayed. If I am in love with God, if I have an intimate loving relationship with God, then I will keep His commands and obey when He speaks to me. When all is said and done, the only way for me to maintain my freedom, be at peace and remain in God so He can remain in me, is to make my love relationship with Him the number one focus of my life. I do not have to worry about trying to remember chapter and verse of all He has told me — even though I do meditate on them — because the Holy Spirit is there to assist me and bring things back to my remembrance. It is the same with the Word of God, it would make no sense memorising the entire bible without having an intimate loving relationship with God.

It is so liberating to be free to live, breath and be intimate with my Lord. God the Father, Son and Holy Spirit have ministered to my inner being, my mind, body and soul.

As I prepare to return home, the physical elements of what is at home may not have changed but I have. I no longer listen to or entertain the devil, I listen to God alone. Last night as I walked with the Lord, the scripture that ministered to me was *"no weapon that is forged against you will prevail."* (Isa 54:17 NIV) And that is what I need to hold unto.

*Father*

*I thank you for the changes You have made and continue to make in me. Father I thank you for loving me enough to send Your only Son Jesus, to die for me. Jesus, I thank you for loving Father enough to obey Him and for loving me enough to go through with it. Your love is amazing! Holy Spirit, I thank You for assisting me, I am relying on You and just knowing You are there to guide me takes the pressure off me trying to remember everything!*

*As I make my love relationship with Father and Son my priority, having You by my side ushering me into Their presence, interceding on my behalf and with me on the behalf of others, is a comfort in itself. This is it. Father live in me, and as I feast on You and all You are, may You overflow from me to others. May others see You in me and desire to know You and give You glory for what You have done and are doing in me. I am the testimony and You will receive the Glory. I declare that the world will know You are God through the lifestyle I lead and may You overflow from the abundance of my heart.*

*My word for today, I am a new creation, old things are passed away and behold all things are made new.*

*I am a new creation.*

# 29

# Hand In Hand Along The Way

When I returned from my first trip back in 2005, I cried uncontrollably, wondering how God could send me back into the real world. I wanted to stay where I was protected, never having to encounter a world outside of His world. It pains me to say it but back then I was still spiritually immature, not that I have reached full spiritual maturity yet. Back then I was so excited about encountering Him the way I did, I felt everything would pan out as my daydreams led me to believe and my dreams took me to faraway places, as I pictured how and when God would bring His promises to pass.

This time around it was different. There were no emotional outbursts but rather a calm undercurrent that held me together. At the airport as I waved good bye to my friend and made my way to the departure gate, I knew that once I stayed under the shadow of the Almighty, I would always feel this safe and secure. Waiting for my plane to depart, I pondered on all God had shown me, taught me and instilled in me. "What if it doesn't all come to pass?" The voice inside me triggered a familiar alarm. Taking a firm stance in my new found security, I shut down the enemy's suggestions and focussed on the reality of God's strength. If God said it would happen, then it would happen, all I needed to do was trust Him. The ownership of how and when it would happen was in His hands, that part of the equation was not my problem. I had no say in the matter; God was in control. After all, it was He who had opened my eyes to all He desired for me. Once I did my part, the emphasis was on God to perform.

Finally, it had hit home, the realisation that all the efforts to make things happen were on God, not me. Once I remained obedient in what He instructed, the completion of the task was His responsibility, not mine. If God ran into problems fulfilling His promise, that was His problem, not mine, He would find a way to make it happen because He is God. Any obstructive wars that took place in heavenly places were not my concern either, they were God's. The beauty of it all was I could rest, confident in the fact that God never struggled, neither did He have any problems fulfilling His promises because there is nothing that can override Him or His Word!

The flight home was peaceful and I was ready to live! Usually when I return home after any trip, my surroundings feel different and I get that feeling, the one that confirms the vacation is well and truly over. Not this time. Being back home felt as if I had only been gone a few hours, like time had stood still. Life at home had remained exactly as I had left it but I had changed.

With my new status came new responsibility. I had to change my approach to God. I no longer came before Him with selfish ambitions of what I needed from our time together but instead it was more of a humble approach, as I sought what was on His agenda. I had to work at changing my mindset so as not to fall back into old habits but the Holy Spirit was with me every step of the way. Some days I had new encounters with God, some days we just sat in silence and some days I got it completely wrong, as I slipped back into my whining rants of "God where are you?" However, I never stayed there for long because the Holy Spirit was there to remind me that that part of my life no longer existed.

Having the Holy Spirit as my guide would be the success of my walk with God, His input in my life was precious.

Returning home, I had no idea how things would pan out, other than the fact that I needed to remain as close to God as possible. I made a point of focussing on my love relationship with Him and left Him to deal with everything else and He wasted no time. Within months, He had made good one of His promises. From a practical perspective, working two days a week, I was in no position to qualify for a mortgage but when your Father rules the universe, you qualify for anything He puts your name on. I arrived home in May and by August I had found a home, got a buyer for a property I owned in Luton that was rented out and secured a mortgage, with no questions asked! God had been faithful and His faithfulness spurred me on to be as faithful to Him as He was being to me. In the space of three months, He had eliminated a major problem that had heavily contributed towards my depression.

Working part time, I had often thought myself powerless regarding certain financial commitments and struggled to trust God entirely with those concerns. Yet He destroyed those concerns, first with His love, followed by His words and actions.

In the midst of moving, I was working on this book and doing all I could to ensure my time with God remained a priority. We must never allow the gifts to overshadow the relationship. We say it over and over but it is true. Putting God first before everything, makes everyday life easier to handle, as everything is seen through His eyes.

Three hundred and seventy four days had passed since I returned home and my experiences with God followed me wherever I went. Back home amidst everyday life, I craved His quiet peace more than ever. I had wonderful days walking hand in hand with my Father and I had tough days when busy schedules kept me away from Him longer than anticipated. For me, the evidence of my growth was now apparent in my everyday life. For one, I had ceased being hard on myself, placing needless pressure upon my small shoulders, hindering God's love from reaching me. I was seeing the manifestation of God's Word develop in the palm of my hands, as they produced things I never thought possible, confirming His words to me *"when I*

***look at you I see a multitude of things you can do."*** I had become more sensitive to my surroundings, that is I was now aware of when I was being led by the Spirit and when I was allowing my flesh to take the lead.

My prayer life had also changed. I loved to sit with Christ and learn from Him. His rest caused my entire being to come to a standstill and hush and I found myself craving quiet time with Him more than I craved my next breath.

God had become my everything. Unless we were ok, I was not ok!

Even after my stupendous trip, I find myself having to work exceptionally hard to maintain an intimate relationship with God. There are no days off. Though my life has changed in many, many ways, my enemy has not changed his tactics but he has stepped up his game. Every so often he tries to throw a curveball, aiming directly at my head in the hope he can knock me off course but thank God for the Holy Spirit!

Being away from my undisturbed solitary place with Father has been challenging for all the right reasons. It is there I see the dramatic changes in my lifestyle. It is there I see the depth of His work within and my love for Him intensifies. It is there I make the choice daily to keep going and though at times I sense old negative familiarities rising within, it is there I choose to hold my head high and walk in God's truth because I have never been as free as I have been since our time together in 2011.

I recall days when my demanding schedule has not allowed me to spend hours in God's presence, as I had grown accustomed to. On those days, the enemy tried his best to condemn me but the very thought of entertaining his lies made me feel sick. Just because my eyes were opened to his tricks did not mean he did not argue a strong case. I had spent two months undisturbed in God's presence. I was accustomed to daily effortless conversations with Him but now there was everyday life, work, starting a business, moving house and a whole heap of surprises that come with renovating a property, to contend with. Some days I felt estranged from God and missed Him terribly but I knew He was with me simply because He told me He would never leave me or forsake me. Some days the enemy tried his hardest to convince me I was going astray because I now had other things occupying my time. Fortunately, the Holy Spirit taught me the beauty of taking ten minutes here and there throughout the day to stop, be still and quieten my spirit so that I could tune into God's surpassing peace, allowing Him to fill my mind, body and soul with His stillness.

Other days, the enemy told me I was a failure because my plate was so full but the Holy Spirit helped me to understand that my time away with God was sacred. It was not possible to remain in the realm I had grown accustomed to 'twenty four seven' but rather something I needed to do frequently. Like Jesus, I had to make time on a regular basis to retire to solitary places, where I could be alone with God for hours or days with no interruptions. During those times, I would glean from Him all I needed before returning back to my everyday duties.

Talk about being love sick! How I missed those endless hours in His presence. However, missing Him is a beautiful thing because it means He is always on my mind and I am always mindful of whose child I am and what is expected of me. Now that does not mean I have not made mistakes, because I have. These have been mainly behavioural slip ups, where I have said something without thinking, complained when I should have kept quiet and the like. Come to think of it, the majority of my slip ups have been centred on my tongue, so I guess I have some work to do there!

Brothers and sisters, God is faithful and unless you are intimately and I stress intimately involved with Him, you are missing out on sensual parts of your relationship with Him. Think of all the conversations He wants to have with you. Think of all the things He wants to show you. The pleasure of entering His rest and being at one with Him — as a child of God, surely you must want this?

I have been a Christian for over thirty years and during that time I have had numerous unnecessary battles with myself, with the devil and with God. All of which have served no purpose other than sleepless nights, endless worry and premature grey hairs. My aim is to eliminate the above by placing my focus where God requires it to be — on Him and I pray you will do the same.

The next time God takes your hand and tries to lead you in a specific direction, follow His lead, regardless of how unnerving it may seem. I do not expect you to take everything from this book and apply it to your lives and never make a mistake again. God does not either but He does expect us to listen to Him, take Him at His word and obey His teachings.

You have a choice, choose wisely!

*Father*

*You love me, You care about me and You have predestined and ordered my steps so that I fulfil the life You created for me. How beautiful are Your plans for my life. Sometimes Your plans, Your strength and Your overwhelming sense of contentment slip my mind and it is then that I realise how naked I am without You.*

*Everyday I encounter the enemy of soul. Everyday he has a new challenge for me. But every morning You shower me with new mercies to see me through that day.*

*How beautiful are Your plans for my life.*

*With love from your daughter.*

I know the plans I have for you
I know just what you're going through
So when you can't see what tomorrow holds
And yesterday is through,
Remember I know,
The plans I have for you
To give you hope for tomorrow
Joy for your sorrow
Strength for everything you go
Through remember I know
The plans I have for you

— MARTHA MUNIZZI —

# 30

# God's Romantic Getaway

When I started this journey, I had no idea where it would lead me but as we draw to a close, my eyes are opened to the beautiful things God wants to show me and do in my life. Having the love of a father is vital and today I am confident I have my Father's love.

Whilst editing the final chapters of this book, I felt God calling me away to spend time with Him and I knew He did not just mean a few hours out of my day. Knowing how precious and special time away with Him can be, I wasted no time in adhering to His call. We were going on another trip and I was excited about the time we would spend together and hoped that the backdrop of the trip would serve as the perfect setting for me to complete the final chapter of the book.

He was taking me back to Orlando and I did not question Him, I just obeyed. The thought of resting in His arms with no interruptions, reminded me of the excitement I felt as a young child approaching the Christmas season. I had the same sort of anticipation as that of opening my gifts beautifully adorned with seasonal wrapping paper beneath the Christmas tree. The kind of excitement that prohibits you focussing on anything else other than what it will be like when you embrace the thing you have longed for.

Being back in the hustle and bustle of life, I craved God's peace and rest, so when He called it was easy to drop everything and follow. The thought of the Florida sunshine greeting me each morning, its warmth penetrating my skin, the silent conversations I would have with God, whilst giving Him my undivided attention. With all that hanging over me, it was hard to concentrate. The trip would last seven days but for all I cared it could have been seven hours. It was not the length of the trip that was important but the fact it was going to be just the two of us. There would be no work, no schedules, no interruption; it would be just me and God in perfect harmony.

After a trying start of early rising and a delayed flight, I arrived in Orlando and amidst my tiredness, I had a burning desire to be in church the following morning.

It was like my body was eager for God's word and my mind was playing catch-up. At church, God's word for me was "Be still and know that that I am God." Be still and listen.

Excellent, I could do that; I could be still and listen. I loved to listen to God. As I drove from church back to my villa, I rested in the assurance that the week was going to be full of spirit filled therapy as God filled me with more of His insights. He had taken me back to the same place we had stayed the previous year, which I thought was touching and thoughtful.

Be still.

Day one was spent sleeping and eating. There was nothing overly spiritual about it. My body needed rest and it needed food, so I gave it what it needed and took delight sleeping in my Father's presence, on the getaway He had planned for me.

Day two was spent in anticipated silence and more sleep, as I awaited His arrival.

Day three was spent walking in the sunshine and taking in the scenery, followed by more sleep and waiting for a word, a whisper or possibly even a kiss from Him. He said to be still and know that He was God. He said to listen and I was listening. The yearning I had for Him was not being filled and I could sense the temptation to welcome failure into the midst hovering all around me. However, I was God's child and God's child did not do failure. If He said He would come, then He would come.

I fought back the arguments accusing me of being lazy and resisted the temptation to complete the last chapter of the book. Prior to the trip, I pictured myself lying prostrate before God night and day, tarrying in His presence as He fed me precious jewels of which I hoped to pass onto you but that was my vision, not His!

Day four came and there was still no word from God. I knew He is there, I could sense Him but for some reason He chose to remain silent. Remembering that it was His trip, not mine, I reminded myself that I could not rush Him; neither could I take the lead. There were a million reasons as to why I was there and in His time, He would speak and make Himself known.

I read, I rested, I ate and I slept. I had no idea my physical body was so tired. I could not take in what He had for me until I was fully rested and free from any attachments back home, so in His loving manner, He allowed me to rest. He knew precisely what I needed and when I was completely empty, I would be where He wanted me to be.

If I am honest, rest is something I welcome, something I never used to get enough of, that was until my last trip. It was there I realised the importance of rest but it was clear that I still had more to learn because as we approached the close of day four, I was still tired and felt like I could have sleep forever. Maybe tomorrow He will sit and speak with me. Maybe He will whisper sweet delights as we walk hand-in-hand. Maybe He will join me on the bench beside the water fountain where I go each day to take in the works of His hand, place His arm around me and hold me so close I will be able to hear His heartbeat. Or maybe He will sit and feed me, while we share a moment together. His ways of reaching out to me are endless, and each brings about a closeness that is breath-taking.

Day five came and I had a wonderful start to the morning. I strolled out of bed, opened the balcony doors and sat watching the sunrise. At 6am, the sun was already warm and singing good morning to the world. My heart was at peace but my mind was wondering whether today would be the day He came because I thought I had this waiting thing down to a T. In a way, I did but had to keep reminding myself not to put God in a box. I felt like I was where I needed to be but I also felt like I should have been doing something. The problem was every time I tried to do something, I began to feel restless, like I was taking charge. It had been a year since I was last here encountering similar emotions, so what had I learned?

Taking a trip down memory lane, I went back to the chapter entitled **Shhh…. Let Him Teach You** and there I found my answer.

The entirety of my last trip had lasted two months and during that time, I had spent one week in Orlando. Throughout the two months, though I had been cut off from distractions, I resided with friends who had been kind enough to open their homes to me but in Orlando, I had been completely alone with God and noticed a shift in the atmosphere. Up until that point, I thought my time away had been special but from the moment I arrived in Orlando, it had been different. My writings spoke of being on a spiritual honeymoon. They spoke of being called away to be still and know God intimately; of being called away to a solitary place to rest in God and with God.

As I read the chapters about my time there, I found my answers and realised that like before, me being back there in the setting I was previously in, was God's Romantic Getaway. It was God's time to have me all to Himself.

There were no scheduled prayer requests, no sackcloth and ashes moments, no spiritual filling station and no desperate calls for help. This was our vacation, God's time to do for me whatever He desired and it would always be centred on me being completely still, so He could have His divine way. I struggled to hold back the tears as I absorbed His divine gift of rest for me. As I began to understand that it was ok to do nothing but rest, I sensed His familiar aroma filling the air.

This was it.

This was our time.

This is what it is all about.

I think I get it now, I think I understand. When Jesus withdrew to solitary places with God, He did it alone and He did it frequently. Aside from those times, we see Him carrying out His role in full time ministry, always talking to the Father and always at work but during those solitary times alone with God, I have to believe He spoke few words, He listened attentively and He rested much. If those times with God, His Father, were not important, there would have been no need to mention it and He would not have done it as frequently as He did.

God's Romantic Getaway is my solitary place with Him. It is the place where EVERYTHING stops for Him; where no schedule places limits on our time together. It is the place where He does what He pleases and I sit back and take it in. Being in the solitary place will always involve lots of rest, so if you are someone that thrives on being busy, you are in for a challenge but I guarantee after your first trip with Him, a hectic lifestyle is something you will shun.

After realising the purpose of my time in Orlando, my last two days were spent at God's pace, which is the most beautiful pace ever because whatever it is you are doing, you find yourself noticing minute details that you would have otherwise overlooked.

Seven days of doing nothing but resting and being still.

Upon my return, when I was asked how my time away was, my response, was 'beautiful,' as I explained I did nothing but rest. It was then that I began to see the beautiful thing God had done for me. He had given me what I needed because coming back, I felt more than rejuvenated. I knew I had been in the presence of the Lord because every time I come back from long periods of time with Him, I find myself doing everything at His pace — a slow, vibrant, confident pace that moves with Godly authority. A pace that is peacefully quiet but not subdued. Another thing I noticed was that my skills had increased. The works my hands produced were of a higher level and as I worked, I realised I had more insight on designs and structure for my work than before. It was evident that in His presence, He had empowered me and this was something He desired to do with me more often.

I had to remind myself that forgetting the former things was something I was still learning. That I was no good to God unless I gave up control over how I thought things should happen. I had to remind myself that there was a vast amount about God that I did not know and I could put a hold on being exposed to more of Him unless I learnt to let go and let God. I had to remind myself that trusting in God meant letting go and until I did so, I did not fully trust Him. All of this and more would be revealed in our time together and I would grow stronger in Him, as I spent time alone with Him.

I had received all this from one week of being still and resting. Many of my revelations had not come whilst I was in Florida but rather, during the first few days of my return home. God was definitely doing a new thing!

On a daily basis, my time with God keeps me in check and enables me to become more sensitive to the leadership of the Holy Spirit. I read about Him and His ways and try my best to implement them in everyday living. On a daily basis, though God is always on my mind, I have to battle with the rude interruptions of my enemy pushing his way into my life; sometimes ignoring the unwanted, unwelcome rebukes. He is so arrogant! On a daily basis, I have to share my time with so many things and balancing so many things can take its toll on my spiritual life as well as my physical life, which is why I now see the importance of the spiritual getaway.

The getaway is something God prompts, a quiet yearning within, for time away with Him. The getaway is His gift to me, allowing me to be in a place where I am sensitive to His voice, benefiting from His way of doing things. From here on in, God's Romantic Getaway will be the vacation we take together. This will be the time when I leave the planning entirely up to Him and all I do is pack my bags and show up, ready to rest uninterrupted in His presence. Knowing this, I am already looking forward to our next trip together. We all know how rejuvenating a vacation can be, so imagine spending a vacation with God. A vacation where He chooses the location, He sets the agenda and everything moves at His pace? I can assure you God's Romantic Getaway will be better than any vacation you have ever taken, the question is — are you ready for it?

This book is full of reasons as to why we need to be completely still before God and I have shared some of my experiences, pitfalls, challenges and the joys of encountering God's stillness. I have spoken of my hunger and thirst for His stillness and the importance of being silent in His presence, thus enabling your body, mind and soul to know Him as God. I have shared some of the ways I entered His stillness and things I did to practice being silent in His presence. I have explained the importance of not knowing everything and explained why we should learn to let go and let God.

I invited you to join me on my journey in the hope it would help you on yours. I have exposed myself to you as God desired. I have cried before you, laughed before you and walked into the unknown before you. I have exposed a fraction of God's never ending love for you and His great mercies. My prayer and hope is that I have introduced you to attributes of God that leave you hungry for more of Him and craving His rest more than ever.

Do not be afraid to step out.

With God by your side, you are in for the time of your life.

*Father*

*As I face everyday life under Your almighty shadow, I find rest in Your arms. You created me. You gave me life and now You desire to take me to higher heights in You.*

*I am not worthy but You made me worthy.*

*I cannot hide anything from You and I am glad that You see and know everything about me. In our times together, You highlight my strengths and encourage me through my weaknesses. You reassure me that I am doing a wonderful job and offer me help where I need it the most. You open my eyes to life and You give me hope in a world full of pain and suffering. I want the world to see the hope You offer.*

*Though I try my hardest, there are days when I will fall but You will be there ready to usher me on and help me overcome. I choose You because I want to live. I choose You because I want to be happy. I choose You because You are the Way, the Truth and the Life. I choose You because You give me hope. Father I choose You.*

*I have friends and loved ones who do not know You but I want them to meet You. I want them to know You as I do. I want them to know what life is. I want the world to know that You save lives because You care about what happens to us. You are not a God of fire and brimstone; You are a God of love. What You have done for me, You have done for many, many others and You desire to do the same for those who are lost. Father help those of us who know You, those of us who are privileged to encounter You in the ways I have, to go out and live a life that draws other to You. Your love is not selfish so ours should not be either.*

*Father thank you for a wonderful life-saving, life-changing year. Thank you for the privilege of sharing part of my testimony but most of all Father, thank you for the Romantic Getaways You have planned for me and those who choose to take You up on Your offer. This is only the beginning.*

*With love from your daughter.*

I've been changed
In the presence of the lord, I've been Healed
freed delivered
In your presence lord I've found joy
Peace, grace
And favour
I won't go back, can't go back, to the way it used to
be Before your presence came and changed me

— WILLIAM MCDOWELL —

*"We are afflicted in every way, but not crushed; perplexed, but not driven to despair; persecuted, but not forsaken; struck down, but not destroyed."* (2nd Cor 4:8–9 ESV)

*"For I know the plans I have for you,"*
*declares the LORD,*
*"plans to prosper you and not to harm you,*
*plans to give you hope and a future."*

JEREMIAH 29:11 NIV

# 31

## After the Getaway

Life after the getaway has been challenging for all the right reasons. It has been far from smooth sailing but most definitely rewarding.

For many years, I bought into the idea that deliverance from depression meant never having to face such feelings again. That after much prayer and God rescuing me, all emotions tied to my depressive traits would disappear without a trace and I would never again succumb to debilitating emotions that sought to kill, steal and destroy my life. Deliverance meant freedom, obliteration and severed ties but when such expectations were not met, I was left discouraged, feeling and believing I would never be free.

In 2011, my world changed and I have tried my best to expla in how much it changed throughout the pages of this book. Even before I returned home, I believed that my forty-year relationship with depression was finally over and in my heart, I purposed to never set eyes on it again but I was wrong, for though deliverance had come and was evident to all who knew me, depression was not far behind on its trail.

My mind-set had changed. The way I viewed things had changed and life continued to come with challenges that in the past, would have sought to transport me back to a place of hopelessness. However, what depression did not realise, was that it would be impossible for me to return to its grasp because the person it once knew no longer existed! Now I knew the truth and the truth was I had the power, mentality, strength and faith to not just fight but to fight and win.

My time spent with God and the continued building of an intimate relationship with Him, caused me to encounter a peace like no other; a peace I could not and would not live without. This peace spurred intimacy and has since become the driving force of my life. It is precious, priceless and I am willing to fight to the death for it. Now, when foreboding feelings of hopelessness or negative connotations come knocking, it is as though I can physically see and feel the heavy weight of oppression that accompany them as they search for somewhere to lay their head, trying to regain their old territory. Choosing to ignore the "NO ENTRY" sign, often they follow me around, attempting to cloud my judgements, hovering, prodding and pushing, in an attempt to bombard their way back into my life, their sole purpose to steal, kill and destroy my peace.

It is amazing what you can see when you have been exposed to the truth. That when embraced, this dark, oppressive cloud will overpower any human being, leaving them for dead in a place of utter despair and hopelessness. Once embraced, it leaves no prisoners, it is all or nothing but I had made a vow that I would never return. Starving the lies and their powerful deceit of the comfort of my mind, I sought — and continue to seek daily — to keep it saturated by what I now know to be the truth, as opposed to what may feel like the 'truth of the day'.

I used to believe I had no control over my emotions, now I knew different. I knew what it felt like to be free and in time, I would know what it felt like to fight and build up emotional and spiritual resistance produced through exercising and putting into practice all I had heard, learned and believed. Now would be my crisis of belief, now would be my testing ground.

Since writing and publishing the first edition of this book, so much has changed. It is as though I am being introduced to the person God predestined me to be. The challenges and curve balls life has thrown have been tough. The lies my mind has whispered seemed real but truth has always prevailed. I have had to run from the heaviness, rebuke the heaviness, dig in deep and make clear it is no longer welcome. Feelings were — and always will be — unreliable; they can change a million times within minutes, so I am learning not to trust anything that does not bring about a deep sense of peace and breathe life. I have learned the true meaning of Jn 10:10, that the thief comes to kill, steal and destroy and brings with him a presence conducive to who he is; likewise my redeemer who gives life and life more abundantly and I choose life. I have learned and continue to learn, that my life is all about choices and if I find myself depressed, it is because of what I have chosen to believe and embrace. That may sound tough but it is the truth.

I have lost loved ones, faced agonising times regarding the health and well-being of my father and become self-employed, the latter being a step of faith that would have never been possible had it not been for the closeness of my relationship with God and my renewed mind-set. I have started a cake company, 'Jemz Cake Box' and launched 'The Annual God's Romantic Getaway 7 Day Retreat'. The retreats centred on intimacy with God, encourages attendees to come away from the distractions of life by following Jesus example of frequently retiring to a solitary place. It is a time of being still and allowing God the time required to minster healing, restoration, rest and direction with no laminations on time. I have also started taking on mentees, as well as speaking at various events and dedicating much needed time to finishing my second book, 'A Precious Stone'.

When you are single, living on your own and you wake up one day to the news of your heavenly Father telling you it is time to give up your main source of income and leave your part-time job, worry and fear are never far behind. Given the opportunity to fester, rest assured, if you have suffered with depression as long as I had, it would not be long before the enemy got on the old bandwagon — and confusion and depression tried to offer unwanted support and counsel. In all fairness, the news to give up my job was not a total shock but I had a mortgage and bills to pay and there was no husband to pick up the tab.

When I asked God how I would manage, He replied "you are going to have to trust Me." Trust with no information equated to blind faith but the sound of His voice alone brought a deep reassurance. It was not the first time He had instructed me to take such a step, neither would it be the last but I knew this time was different. Though I had no idea of what the next step would be or how I would manage financially, what I was sure of was I would never be employed by someone again and God was most definitely speaking to me.

It took a different level of faith but His Godly presence that always guided me in such situations, was always near. When you take a step by faith, knowing with all confidence what you are about to do is from God and without Him as the orchestrator, you know the backlash of your actions would be disastrous, you cannot help but walk strong and stay close as you recognise His ever familiar signature, 'Peace'. That Peace that surpasses all natural understanding. That Peace that calms every thought before it arises, that Peace that says "I am with you". That Peace that lets you know that if you do not obey, the consequences far outweigh the uncertainty of the unknown. By consequences, I do not mean God punishes you, He is not like that. What I mean is that each step of faith we take is a step to another level. Just as when you climb a flight of stairs, each step takes you to another level and brings you closer to the top, so it is with our steps of faith. Every time you obey a direct instruction from God, you move up a level.

Have you ever climbed a flight of stairs that started out easy but the closer you got the top, your legs became tired and started to ache? The brisk quick step you started off with slowly turns into you hanging onto the banister rail, breathing heavily and pausing longer, as you commit to making it to the top? It is the same with our faith; each step of faith we take with God, pushes us further out of our comfort zone. It chips away at our carnal mannerisms and strengthens our weak belief system. It instigates growth in our Christian walk, whilst strengthening our relationship with God. Failure to comply, whatever the reasons, leaves us at the bottom of the stairs or midway, looking up, desiring to reach the top but stagnant in a place of doubt and fear; and doubt and fear are the perfect breeding ground for the enemy.

Truth is, when you have an *intimate* relationship with God, emphasis on intimate, you come to expect requests that are out of the ordinary, simply because God is far from ordinary. Intimacy with God is where my strength lies and the key to understanding His ways as much as is humanly possible without wanting to know everything and always allowing His peace to guard my heart and mind.

Provided God is doing the leading, I have found walking into the unknown to be one of the safest places in the world. Such reassurance does not stem from you praying about something you want to do and telling God to come on board. No, it stems from God gently pushing you to the next staircase and saying, "Okay, my child, it is time to climb."

It is the reason why on 1st October 2014, a month after handing in my notice, I woke up to my first day of no job and no plans, just faith and a deep sense of peace. I did not feel at peace; I was at peace and my peace was evidence that God was near and His presence was guiding me. To not sense His peace was to take my eyes off Him and this was easy to recognise because it left me exposed to worry and doubt, something I could not be a part of. Using an analogy of animals in nature, God showed me a mother lioness pushing her young cubs out into the wild and I remember thinking how cruel it was to do such a thing to such cute looking cubs and though further on down the line it was evident why she had done it, initially it did not stop me wishing she could have kept them safely tucked away at her side. It was then that God said *"this is what I am doing with you. What I am asking you to do may feel uncomfortable but it is the only way I can get you to grow, to find out what you are made of and who you are."* And that is precisely what life after the getaway has consisted of me being introduced to the person who always was but had never been given the opportunity to surface.

It has been about accepting who I am in Christ, walking in my purpose and facing the obstacles, of which there have been many, with a new mind-set. It has been about standing on God's words and not returning to one's old self. Life after the getaway has been rewardingly hard work, it has involved coming face to face with the enemy and refusing to give in. Seeking God in prayer and making time for Him. Building on my intimate relationship with Him and regularly retreating to a solitary place. Incorporating scheduled times of prayer and fasting into my Christian walk. Bringing my flesh into subjection with the Word of God. Consciously making decisions to live by the Word and to live by faith and not by sight. It has meant sometimes watching the very thing God said would live, die, yet with a defiantly made-up mind, refusing to accept death, knowing He is the Resurrection and the Life. It has been about getting militant in my walk and taking authority over my life. Encouraging myself in the Lord and pushing through the tears to achieve triumphant personal joys. It has been lonely at times and painful as I have learned to push, push, push and never give in or give up.

Have I felt like giving up? I have felt tired and weary and I have heard the suggestive voice of the enemy willing me to give up but giving up is not an option because that choice has no life attached to it and when faced with the choice, I chose life! I chose life and the enemy set himself up to steal it. When things spiralled out of control, he was there, when financially things got tough, he was there. When book sales were low, he never ceased to remind me, offering me my bed and warm duvet stacked with oppression for comfort. But I learned how to get tough and found the Holy Spirit never left me once I kept my eyes on Him. It was ok to cry but not for long because on numerous occasions, I actually heard him say *"ok, enough crying, what are you going to do now?"* And with the question came a choice, I could get up and move on to plan B, C, D, E or whichever letter of the alphabet I was on, not always knowing what the outcome would be but knowing I was gaining ground, or I could give in to hopelessness. The thought of giving in to hopelessness made me feel sick, angry and frustrated. It robbed me of life, determination to succeed and the ability to dream. It robbed me of perseverance and most of all, my peace. I work hard at remaining focussed, I ride out the waves of unstable emotions and I do so through my relationship with God and as a result, I am gaining strength from the well of life rising within.

It has been no 'walk in the park' but gaining victory over my emotions and old mind-set, has fuelled my freedom. I now understand why Paul was able to go through and feel the pangs of hardship, yet still write and preach the way he did. It all comes down to your intimate, personal relationship with God and choosing to stand your ground, regardless. At some point in your life, you have to make a decision to no longer be the person described in James 1:6–8 (NIV) *But when you ask, you must believe and not doubt, because the one who doubts is like a wave of the sea, blown and tossed by the wind.7 That person should not expect to receive anything from the Lord. Such a person is double-minded and unstable in all they do.*

When things get tough, I reinforce my decision to trust God and follow what His Word says, I reinforce my decision to trust all He has said to me and though my flesh suffers as a result, in the end, my Spirit gains strength and I win!

To date, my life has been about winning the battles I am faced with, as opposed to cowering away under the oppression of lies fed to me. My greatest achievement since 2011, has been my personal growth and being able to inspire others who have walked and continue to walk in the shoes I once wore. Not only them but those who are weary, tired, battle with fear, doubt or feel weak in their Christian faith. Whether in passing, mentoring, speaking or hosting my retreats, I cannot help but share my testimony of how I went from being an indecisive, depressive mess, on the verge of a mental breakdown to a fighting, winning child of God. How I went from struggling to believe and trust God, to being unable to doubt Him. How hearing His voice and intimacy with Him, has become the number one pursuit of my life because everything changes when Papa speaks.

I love and am encouraged at the transformation in the lives of both believers and non-believers that attend the God's Romantic Getaway Retreats. How they too come to the point where intimacy with God is something they crave more than their next breath and the way in which they, in turn, share with others. It truly is a domino effect and one I pray will continue until God's will be done on earth, as it is in heaven.

*Father*

*These past few years have pushed me to what I believe at times have been my limit, yet You show me there is always more and I am stronger than the enemy would have me believe.*

*My life has changed in so many ways and though sometimes it feels like I am fighting more than I am resting, I will fight with every ounce of strength You give me to hold on to what I have found and continue to experience in and with You.*

*I am Your child, created in Your image. You have given me authority to overcome all the wiles of the enemy because You have already defeated him. So Father, thank you for Your patience, Your guidance, Your strength. Thank you for Your words of wisdom, insight, knowledge and understanding. Thank you for those moments of intimacy which have become the driving force of my life. Thank you for the lives that have been touched and continue to be touched by You through my obedience and the testimony of what You have done and continue to do in my life. Father, thank You for life and life more abundantly. Thank you for helping me to recognise Your support as I go through the storms, for realising that removing me from the firing line does not always work in my favour; sometimes I need to go through the fire in order to come out stronger.*

*Father thank You for being more than a Father, more than a friend, more than a lover, for being EVERYTHING I need in order to live a spiritually abundant life.*

*Father thank you for saving my life.*

*With love from your daughter.*

*Amen.*